T0113813

A Two Week Notice

Chuck Stories

Chuck Barrett

WESTBOW
PRESS®
A DIVISION OF THOMAS NELSON
& ZONDERVAN

WestBow Press books may be ordered through booksellers or by contacting:

WestBow Press
A Division of Thomas Nelson & Zondervan
1663 Liberty Drive
Bloomington, IN 47403
www.westbowpress.com
1 (866) 928-1240

ISBN: 978-1-5127-3956-5 (sc)
ISBN: 978-1-5127-3957-2 (hc)
ISBN: 978-1-5127-3955-8 (e)

Library of Congress Control Number: 2016906604

Print information available on the last page.

WestBow Press rev. date: 04/29/2016

"Chuck Barrett is the master story-teller as he reflects over more than 20 years of missionary service in Africa. His graphic description of cross-cultural experiences are filled with humor and emotion. For anyone interested in missions, "A Two Week Notice" will inspire with accounts of God's faithfulness and timely guidance in the journey of obedience."

Jerry Rankin, President Emeritus
International Mission Board, SBC

I can't count the number of times I have been asked "What did you do all those years serving in Africa?" Chuck has recorded the "good and the bad" and in a few experiences "the ugly" of living on mission in a cross-cultural setting. Chuck and Alicia's experiences remind me of Romans 12:1 from "The Message." Petersen writes it, "Take your everyday, ordinary life—your sleeping, eating, going-to-work, and walking-around life—and place it before God as an offering. Embracing what God does for you is the best thing you can do for him." Chuck explains that ordinary life in Malawi, South Africa and Australia. This enjoyable read covering the variety of experiences illustrates the ordinary life of a cross-cultural worker. In that context you see again and again the Lord's presence and ministry of drawing people to Himself. A great read!

Jon Sapp
Retired IMB Regional Leader
Central, Eastern and Southern Africa

Being a veteran missionary myself, I thoroughly enjoyed reading A Two-Week Notice

For those of us dedicated to ministry, Chuck Barrett's honest, down to earth approach will surely inspire and challenge you.

For those who would like deeper insights into a missionary's calling, preparation, challenges and field experiences, Chuck Barrett will not disappoint.

Chuck will take you on a delightful journey from the U.S. to Africa to Australia. There is much food for thought in these pages. You will laugh and you will cry but I will predict, when you reach the last page you will definitely want to read more stories from Chuck.

Bill Viser, Ph.D.
Professor of Christian Ministries
Ouachita Baptist University

"Each person's journey of faith is part of the sequel to the book of Acts! In this book, Chuck Barrett shares his calling and missions experience through his daily walk of obedience as he encounters individuals and situations that both challenge and affirm his faith. Chuck demonstrates that it is in the moment by moment living of life that we encounter the living Christ."

Ian Cosh
Vice President for Community and Int'l. Engagement
Ouachita Baptist University

CONTENTS

INTRODUCTION

I HAVE BEEN ENCOURAGED AT several points to put some of my stories in a format that could be shared. These encouragements came in differing forms, from various sources, and for a variety of reasons. Regardless, I've appreciated the spurring. This is just an attempt to get that request started. I really wish you could meet the people I did, as I did, but as that is not possible, I have changed or not used names of many friends and colleagues to protect the innocent—and myself from libel. If you find yourself within these stories, I hope they bring back fond memories or perhaps a string of memories.

CHAPTER 1

The Beginning

I CANNOT REMEMBER A TIME in adult life when I was not involved in ministry somehow, somewhere, except for a brief time, when starting both college and seminary, where we were looking for a church home. Prior to Alicia and I getting married, we both felt a pull to missions, and we joined several other families at the start of Orchards Baptist Church in Loveland, Colorado.

Soon after our marriage, I was prompted by the Lord to get an education. This came at a time when I was working in Colorado as a warehouse manager of a small subsidiary of a large oil company. I was driving to work, conversing with my Lord, when I asked if this was what He wanted me to do with my life. I received the answer that I needed: pursue a college education. I returned home to share with Alicia what I believed the Lord had told me. The next thing I knew, she had enrolled me in university and we were moving to Greeley, Colorado, to begin the next stage of our journey.

We only moved seventeen miles to the east, yet I knew relationships would change. One man in particular held a very dear place in my heart: my best man, boss for a time, and one of my spiritual heroes, Rod W. I prayed one simple prayer as we left town that day, which has had, in hindsight, a significant impact on my journey since: "Lord, give me a love for all men like you have given me for this man." That prayer, perhaps more than any other, changed my life in ways I may never know and certainly didn't know at the time. I believe that without this small prayer, and without God answering this prayer throughout our journey, we would not have seen, known, and loved all the people we have along the way. You may have heard it said, "If you don't want to hurt so badly, don't love so deeply." We, as many, have dealt with the choice to love deeply. There are stories of many lives that have touched ours—men and families with whom we have shared life and struggles, both physical and spiritual—that could fill volumes; we recall each fondly. These are not all of the stories, just a smattering from along the way.

Suffice it to say, I did finish college quickly, but at a time when jobs were few and far between. I did find work, and that is exactly what it was: w-o-r-k. Again, I asked the Lord if this is what He had in mind when prompting me to college. His words to me were very clear, though vague: I could do what I was doing for Him, but overseas—whatever that meant. Again, I went home to tell Alicia exactly what I had prayed and received from the Lord. She knew immediately what to do (I still need to learn what not to say to my wife).

Over the next several months, I found myself filling out paperwork for the Foreign Mission Board (FMB) of the Southern Baptist Convention (SBC): medical questionnaires, statement of faith, bio-sketch, and on it went. After I had written about all I could stand to write, we received job requests in the mail! I was trained and educated in the business field, so I felt all the jobs would be about the same. So when Alicia called with the list of requests sent to us (there were only three), I told her I didn't need to know the job, just the place. There was some discussion about that, but the place God laid on my heart was Salima, Malawi. Malawi is a small land-locked country in southeastern Africa. Who knew? But I get way ahead of myself.

So, here we are, looking at this clinic administrator job request for Salima, Malawi, and our hearts are filling with joy and excitement. We placed the request on hold after Alicia had a conversation with a veteran missionary from Zambia, a neighboring country to Malawi. Two weeks later, the news came to us that an oversight had been made, and we were not qualified for the job in Malawi as it had the requisite of a religious master's degree. Heartbroken, we pressed on, knowing that God had called us, and He was in control. We went back to the other two requests we had received. We placed one of those on hold and proceeded through the necessary stages of appointment.

It came time for us to go to Richmond, both for candidate consultation and physicals. I recall this particular October morning in Richmond, Virginia, was chilly, but the air-conditioning was still on at the doctor's office. I must have been blue by the time he walked in! I was frozen to the examination table as I had obeyed the nurse's instruction to strip down. His head down, reading my chart while he entered the room, the doctor took one look at the country we had selected and mentioned something about the heat there. I could not hold my tongue and said that anything was better than my current condition. At this he took notice of me, apologized for the temperature of the room, and began treating me for hypothermia.

We also had to go see a psychologist to receive his all-clear. We had gone with another couple just to have some time to chat and get to know each other, so when the doctor opened his office door to call his next appointment in, he was a bit shocked that there were four of us and not the usual two. When he called each of us in, he literally only stuck his bald head out of the doorway, so we had no idea he suffered from the effects of polio. When he called for me, I joined him in the hallway behind the door, and I could now see the twisted, braced body attached to that bald head as he invited me to "walk this way." Of course, I did. He had a great sense of humor.

To make a longer story shorter, we left Richmond not filling that request—not because of what I did or didn't do, as some have accused, but with the advice that we should wait two years before contacting the FMB again. We left, as you can imagine, defeated and confused. Had we missed something? Had God indeed spoken? With these questions and others, we returned to the routine with which we were more than familiar. Then the most amazing thing happened.

CHAPTER 2

The First Two-Week Notice

I RETURNED FROM WORK JANUARY 7, 1992, a day that will be etched in my mind for as long as I may have one, to find Alicia waiting for me at the door with one of those looks. Young, married men may know the look of which I speak. Only two things could bring this look: one, she's scheming or two, she's expecting. I didn't have to wait long. "If," she said, already hyperventilating, "I could sell our house, sell my car, pack us up, get you enrolled in seminary, and find us a place to live, would you consider starting seminary this next semester?"

No need to say I was looking for an escape hatch, so I replied, "When does the next semester start?"

She didn't miss a beat. "The twentieth."

"Of *this* month?" was my logical question.

She responded with a simple yes and an ongoing Cheshire cat kind of smile, awaiting my reply. What was I to do? I knew in the kind of housing market that faced us it could not happen that quickly, so I said, "Sure."

Well, if you know my wife, you can guess, it happened—it all happened. I had to give two weeks' notice! Two weeks' notice is perhaps another theme that runs through our missionary journey, but something to keep in mind is that I was blessed and am blessed. I don't recall packing the rental truck, probably because I wasn't there and my best friend in the world packed my stuff for me. Sunday, January 19, 1992, we were packed in our moving van, and after church, we headed for Kansas City, Missouri, to begin our seminary journey at Midwestern Baptist (MBTS).

Perhaps one of those unmentionable aspects of our calling is all the tearful, painful good-byes along the way. While on our first return to the States after our first term in Malawi, I jokingly reflected that I left my family, my friends and even Walmart. Well, Walmart was not that tearful of a good-bye for me, but I'm told it has been for some. I knew with each transition that my prayer to love all men was becoming real. But again, I get ahead of myself.

I've never stopped to thank Steve and Debbie, nor am I sure of their last name, but as we were driving I-70 late Sunday evening—it could have been early Monday morning—they rescued us. Alicia and I were busy dreaming and discussing our hopes for the future and what life back in school would be now that we had two young children in tow … so busy talking, in fact, neither of us noticed the fuel levels as the sun was setting. By the time my attention was drawn to our fuel shortage, the *idiot* light was illuminating our dire situation. On I-70 east of Salina, Kansas, there is just not much, especially in the dark. I saw a sign on the highway for Alma and turned right, and kept heading right. There in the darkness, after what seemed many miles, we found Alma sleeping, blissfully unaware of us (I bet some of you wish that). Behind us on the road came a custom van, which made the stop behind us at the intersection. I went back to ask for assistance. Inside were Steve and Debbie returning from celebrating Steve's fortieth birthday. We were invited to follow them to the Stonewall Cafe, of which they were proprietors. Steve contacted the owner of the local gas station to see if he would assist us while Debbie brewed coffee. We enjoyed a great conversation over coffee while the gas station owner was driving to and opening his shop.

I don't know if these kind folks remember that one simple act for these weary strangers, but it made a world of difference. Who knows where we would be without their kindness. We were back on the road at around 1:30 a.m. and arrived at the MBTS about five that morning; introductory classes started at eight. We unpacked bare essentials, met the neighbors who opened our house for us, and curled up on the floor for a few hours rest.

I really hate to disappoint people or shatter their views of the world about as much as I like having mine shattered. One of the great dreams of seminary that occupied our minds along the journey toward Kansas City was meeting so many men of the caliber of our pastor. Should that not have been our expectation? Well, we were, needless to say, disappointed. They were all just folks like me! Now you too are greatly disappointed!

CHAPTER 3

Mosby, Missouri

WHILE A NEW STUDENT AT MBTS, I was assigned a group of peers (coming later in life with family in tow) with whom to meet. I still consider each one a friend, but one friend, Steve Cazzell, remains closest to my heart. We arrived with no knowledge of larger city life, and we began to church shop. Many of you know what that is: "Let's find a church that suits us." We were not very successful, and for three months, we searched. During this time, Steve constantly invited me to his church, some thirty-five miles away from the seminary. I just could not see Alicia and I driving that far, as she worked in the city, and we lived on campus, so it was just a walk for me to classes. Our children's care provider lived in the next duplex, and we were in a great situation; why would I want to change that? Steve persisted until I finally broke down. We were to travel to Mosby from Kansas City for a praise sing at the Mosby Baptist Church.

We were identified as visitors immediately, as we used the front door rather than side door. It was cold, the sun setting quickly as winter was not yet over, and as we walked through the doors, a sense of being home came over us. Unless you have experienced such a feeling, it is hard to describe. We took our seats as Steve's mother, Betty, led the singing, calling for requests of favorite hymns. I took the bait and made my request. I was then asked to come up and lead it. Oh, I should have seen that train coming. We were hooked.

I do need to share that our time with Mosby was wonderful in other ways as well. Steve had prepared the way for us, and folks knew we were in the area preparing for life as missionaries in an overseas setting. The church offered to employ me to lead worship and work with youth. Money was not the draw for the ministry there, and it's a good thing, but it did cover our fuel expenses. Our journey also provided the church with their own missionary, an honor that touches my heart deeply at every remembrance.

We fell in love with the people and the community. I do have to say that Mosby is a forgotten little town in the flood plain of the Fishing River and had passed its prime. The Baptist church was the only worship center in town. The post office was kept open, perhaps out of pity, but was just a small garden-shed-sized building. My friend Steve was the volunteer fire chief; the only fire crew the town had was volunteer. His wife Julie was town clerk. The school had been closed, and the children were bussed to Excelsior Springs for all grades. There was not even a convenience store in town. Though technically the filling station and attached shop were in the town, they were strategically placed between the north and southbound lanes of the freeway. This just to say Mosby was not a thriving metropolis, but we loved it. We loved it so much we just had to move there, so we left campus and made our drives in every day. That may say more about our mental state than leaving the convenience of Walmart for Malawi. The next year and a half was spent in beautiful relationship with Mosby and its people.

Too many events and so many people from Mosby still hold our hearts that it would be a shame to try and write about them all, but there are a few I have to share. We were celebrating Labor Day with the church family by having a barbecue at the Cazzell homestead, Steve's parents' place, when a call came from the firehouse. There was a barn burning and the Fishing River Fire Department needed to respond immediately. Steve asked if I wanted to join him in the small command truck while the other volunteers kitted up and met up with us in the pump truck. I assured him I would enjoy that, and away we went. As we crested the hill to allow for our first view of the burning barn, I said, "I don't know what you've got, but it isn't big enough." We could only ensure the fire did not spread from where it was started as large, round bales of hay lay fully engulfed in white-hot flames.

Then there was the evening one of the elderly women in the church came to say how upset she was with me as I had never come for pie. Pie! Sweet pie is nothing like a Cornish pie or steak and kidney pie, which I would later not mind. I assured her of my ignorance to her desire that I come for pie. "It was a standing invitation for every Sunday evening after church services," she said. We went that evening! I took the entire family! We knocked on Lena's door and were invited in warmly and told to make ourselves at home. She then asked what pie we wanted. Alicia and I looked at each other, and then at the children. It was, after all, Sunday evening, and though pie is great, we just knew we didn't have the time for this sweet woman to create and bake one pie, let alone if someone wanted a different pie. It was as if she saw through our private musings when she said, "I have seven pies ready," listed them, and then asked again which pie would we like.

We made our selections. "Apple for me, please, Lena," I said quickly. Knowing she had three cream pies, Alicia chose her favorite. Now, we learned who this woman was. Lena was the retired chief chef for the school. She loved to bake, and she always had a minimum of seven varieties of pie ready. Then we learned how pies were served! Did you know that a nine-inch pie was only meant to serve four! I didn't know that either. When seminary was finished, we rolled out of Mosby.

Robert and Barbara Kenny became dear friends during our seminary days. They say folks will come to church out of relationship, regardless of the distance. Because of our time with Mosby and Robert and Barbara, I know it's true. Robert was very soft-spoken, never a hair out of place, and deliberate with every movement; Barbara, not so much. We joined the seminary bowling league to get to know some of our fellow seminarians and to enjoy a night out. We arrived early and chose our team by who was next through the door; they had to be at least as excited as we were. It was Robert and Barbara. Robert walked in as if he could walk out at any moment, and Barbara came in as if she were entering the children's play area. Alicia and I looked at each other, knowing these folks would not be a fit, but we stuck to our guns. The ice was really broken when Robert threw a strike, and I put my hand up to give him a high five. Okay, my hand was in front of Alicia's face, but it was quick, and he didn't notice. So, as he made the move to slap my hand, I pulled mine away—how immature of me—and he made contact with Alicia's forehead. His reaction still causes laughter. Not much later, Robert had just dipped his newly purchased corndog into mustard and was about to take a bite when Alicia helped it along! Friendships, go figure. Ours became one of a lasting variety.

During our second trip to Richmond, Virginia, Robert and Barbara stayed with our children in Mosby. I did say Mosby was on the floodplain of the Fishing River. While we were in Richmond, rains fell, and the river rose, causing the need for evacuation. I'm not quite sure our children ever fully recovered from that trauma. The dog was only remembered the next day, but she too was fine … just a bit of excitement. We returned to find Robert was not well, as he had spent much time in the heat and humidity cleaning our car of any sign of the flood.

The lawnmower was flooded and needed an overhaul before being used. One afternoon I stuck myself into the job without changing into something I could really work in and get dirty. I took the motor apart, cleaned it, and put it back together. It was time for a trial start! It did. I was not one to test my work and give it another start. It was working; it should be used, and the grass was over a foot tall! Still in dress clothes, I took off for the backyard and then the front yard, still going strong! Steve's yard needed mowing too! Off I went. As Alicia was getting home, so was I. She was more concerned about my wardrobe choice than excited about a working lawnmower. The lawnmower kept working until we left.

Perhaps just one more story. We were back in Mosby for a visit after our first term of service in Malawi, when Steve and his brothers introduced me to potato guns! That may say more about me than I really want you to know. I was thrilled! One of Steve's brothers had made this particular gun and painted it camouflage. It was perfect. Potato guns have no real practical application that I can think of; they're just an enjoyable past-time. The Cazzell men gave me that gun, but it would not fit into a suitcase, so I had to cut the barrel. I bought the necessary coupling and glue, and packed it for Malawi. It was never really questioned as it was PVC and posed no real threat. Yet bring that bazooka-looking thing out at dusk, load it, fire it, and you have an amazing intimidator, with the blue flames from the muzzle and the following deep thud of the explosion. I just enjoyed the reminiscing.

CHAPTER 4
The Call: Salima, Malawi

WE HAD, PERHAPS, A DIFFERENT call process to missions than others, experiencing first that call on our hearts to cross cultural barriers to ministry, and then a call to a specific place. When we arrived in Kansas City and I began classes at MBTS, we were contacted by the FMB. They simply said, "We did not authorize this move." We were shocked! We didn't ask for any input. We could only say that we were following where we believed God was leading in our lives. The response was, "Well, that job will probably not be open by the time you are ready to fill it." Along the journey, we've learned we are not responsible for the outcome of our obedience. As Charles Stanley said, "Obey God and leave all the consequences to Him."

In the process, we were allowed to contact the FMB and place a job on hold when we were less than a year from being able to go to the field. After a year of seminary and just a year from being able to go to the field, we contacted the FMB again to see if the Salima, Malawi, job was still open. To our delight, it was! We placed the job on hold, and as the candidate consultant assigned to the seminary was visiting campus, I asked, "Is the job on hold for us?"

He causally responded, "Chuck, that job has been on hold for you for a long time." Seems some guy in Richmond, Virginia, that is the namesake of our youngest placed a sticky note on the job request that read, "Chuck and Alicia Barrett, good match."

What Lies Ahead

We were in Richmond again when the flooding returned to the Fishing River and Mosby, Missouri. We were getting answers to so many questions and learning so much about what lay ahead. I knew the mission station that we were going to had not had any career missionaries attached to it for several years. I was presented with the opportunity to ask the associate for our region in Richmond, "When we land, are they going to plop five years of paperwork on my desk and say, 'Welcome to Malawi?'"

"Oh, no," he said with a slight sardonic chuckle. "You have to go through language school first." There are times I hate sarcasm.

Just so you are aware, we did have to redo physicals and psychological testing, this time with a different medical staff, including a psychologist. He invited us into his massive office with multiple seating options and simply said, "Take a seat." I sat in the center of the sofa against the wall, sensing my selection of seat in itself was some sort of psychological indicator. After his questions, he asked if I had any questions. Well of course I did.

"Am I normal?" I asked.

His simple response continues to say it all: "Do you want to be normal?"

The First Challenge

Alicia and I were so excited about the future. We had nearly completed seminary, and we had the original Salima, Malawi, request on hold. We were scheduled for our training time before we left the United States. In fact, we were already packed, and it was nearly Christmas when my father-in-law unexpectedly arrived on our doorstep. I was taken aback, to say the least, as too many questions flooded my mind. "What are you doing here, and where is your wife?" were the two big questions left unasked at the time. "Come on in," I said as I looked out the front door to see if my mother-in-law was still in the car. I had heard he was taking a trip to the southwestern part of Missouri, but just why I don't think anyone but he knew. We exchanged the usual greetings, and finally I addressed the elephant in the room.

"What are you doing here?" And with excitement, he began to show me photos. He carefully aligned 4x6 pictures on my dining table, creating a panoramic view of a sloping countryside.

"That's pretty," I said. "What is it?"

"I'm glad you asked!" was to be his catchphrase for this conversation. "This is a cattle ranch I just bought in southwestern Missouri!"

In disbelief, I asked, "How are you going to run a cattle ranch in southwestern Missouri when you live in Colorado?"

"I'm glad you asked! Are you sure God has called you to Africa?"

It was beginning to sink in, but I was slow. "Yes," I said, still unaware of where he had planned for the conversation to go.

"But," he continued, "God could change His mind."

Then, warnings of all types began to go off in my mind as I caught just what was cooking in the head of this cost accountant. "Yes," I said. "God could change His mind."

"Are you sure you wouldn't rather run a cattle ranch right here in Missouri?"

Wow, of all the places the first distraction could come from, this one was not even on my radar. Here I was taking this man's only daughter and—sorry to the rest of you, but I am biased—his best grandchildren all the way over to Africa! Who was I? What did I think I was doing? Yet I knew God had called, cleared the way, and made every provision for the journey thus far. How could I slam the door now? I treasure the picture that was taken that day in our little house in Mosby, Missouri. It is of a very excited yet confused young couple with packed footlockers up against the wall in the background, filled with what we felt necessary for the journey ahead. Yet behind the camera stood a man who was looking at four of his greatest treasures ready to take flight so far away from one who held them so dear.

Another brother-in-law shared his insight with me. "If you love something, let it go. If it doesn't return to you, hunt it down and shoot it!" Chester, I love you.

Saying good-bye to Dad/Grandpa

CHAPTER 5

Malawi

We're Not in Kansas Anymore

WE FLEW OUT OF RICHMOND in the cold, bleak grays and whites of winter. We landed for a brief, torturous layover in Paris. Needless to say, the weather in Paris was cold, gray, and bleak. We boarded an Air France 747 bound for Lilongwe, Malawi! Wow! At last! What to expect, who would greet us, what would we do our first day? When the doors of that 747 opened, we stepped, sleep deprived and travel weary, into the sauna of the Malawi rainy season. It was the kind of heat that takes your breath away the moment it engulfs you. Remember, we left in the dead of winter, mid-March. The ice storms we had encountered closed the nation's capital for days. We were moving to the southern hemisphere, where seasons are opposite. I was carrying the family's winter coats, and the easiest way to carry mine was to wear it. The overwhelming heat, as well as the brilliant colors, flooded my mind and body. "We're not in Kansas anymore."

Language School

Language school, a time of adjusting like no other, provides opportunity for the testing and trying of everything within each of us. During language school, the depth of every individual and couple's calling, faith, patience, and commitment, is tested. Is it any wonder why this is often known as language torture?

For those wondering what language school is like, lock yourself in a room with strange smells, different foods, and a language learning tape playing. Now, bring in a friend who understands that language to translate and perhaps a few of his friends who also speak the language so you can practice. See, the thing is, regardless how hard one may try, there is still an out. You are still home; you still go out to get your favorite meal or go to your favorite shop. And if friends and family are close, you enjoy their company. For people serving in a foreign field of service, those comforts have been removed, and you are each other's only support system. Close relationships with colleagues need to be built quickly, but who do you trust? Close friendships took time to develop back home, time that mission personnel often don't have if they are to survive in their new environment.

I don't know if it is true, but we felt as though we were being weighed on the scales as soon as we arrived: if we would stay or run; if we were keepers. I'd have to do some investigation into this question, but I'm not sure I'd like the information I uncovered, so I'll leave that task undone; another goal met! I do know after we had some years of experience, we could see the bitter battle in other's lives and wonder these things.

We lived in Malawi's capital of Lilongwe for language school, which provided both challenges and opportunities. We would wake on the average weekday and have breakfast, which was normally prepared by our house worker. That was strange, getting used to having someone in the house cooking for you and cleaning up after you. After breakfast, we would take the children to their school, named after Dr. David Livingstone's son-in-law, Bishop Mackenzie. Then we'd head toward the Baptist Theological College, which required us to cross the river. Our teacher was Mr. Phiri, which translates to Mountain. We had some time to discuss our practice the day before and ask questions that would arise out of the previous day's conversations. Then we would get our answers and the next phase or phrase for the conversation, some grammar, and some cultural learning. From the classroom, we would go to Lilongwe's central market to practice what we had learned. We found the bean vendors in the center of the market most helpful. Alicia could practice with the ladies, and I could practice with the men. The market was very casual, calm, and clean ... well, two out of three. Our tutors could still sell beans and talk to us, so we were not a major interruption, but a welcome distraction. Our language mistakes provided humor for our hosts, frustration for us, and fodder for teaching the next day's class.

The bean vendors proved to be most helpful. They also proved to be great friends. We had to walk into the inner court of the market to reach the bean vendors, so we passed nearly every other vending stall to reach them. The market was large and crowded. It was also not the most hygienic environment, though you could buy anything from buttons to goat heads. The toilets were not always convenient to use, so sewage was channeled through a trench that ran through the market, increasing the brutal attack on the sensory system. It did not take long for everyone to recognize who we were, where we were going, and what we were doing. As familiarity with us rose, so did conversation and jesting. As our ability to converse grew, so did our relationships, and it was a great shame that just as we were getting to know each other, we had to move to our station of service. Later, when Mom and Dad came to Malawi for a visit, I took Dad back to my bean vending friends. It was a joy to see Dad going through what I had just two years prior. The market was unlike any market he had experienced previously. Upon returning to the house, he told Mom, "Chuck took me to the market." Mom was sure there were markets just like that when she was a young girl going to the farmer's markets in southeastern Kansas. Dad simply assured her the two markets were nothing alike!

Charmed

Several events from our language school time are memorable. One of these is the time I found traditional charms at each corner of the house. I was just enjoying the garden and the flowers that were new to me when I noticed a bit of ribbon in the flower bed at one corner of the house. I reached down and discovered a bit of corncob tied by the ribbon to a chicken feather. I kept walking around the house to see if this was the only thing of its kind. I found a different thing at each corner of the house. One was a chicken foot tied by ribbon to tree bark; chicken parts and plant parts tied with ribbon was the theme. I gathered these up and took them to a smaller local market where we often practiced our language skills in the afternoons.

The woman at the market, who knew we were Christian, asked where I found these items. I told her at the corners of our house. I asked what they meant, and what their significance was. She informed me that she believed they could mean anything depending on who placed them. She then advised me to put them back where I found them. The woman said that whatever the reason for the placement of these charms, their removal would be more detrimental than just leaving them alone. I was skeptical, but knowing my God was bigger than any charm or the power of that charm reassured me of their powerlessness. I put them back.

When you are new to a culture, there are many strange things, not all of which must be understood, as this cultural teacher informed us. She may have actually known the purpose of these charms, but for our peace of mind, left us ignorant. Sometimes, ignorance *is* bliss. I slept well in the house as long as we lived there.

But I Was Speaking English!

We were in need of a mop to clean the floors of the house. You would think everyone would know what I was looking for—after all, everyone cleans their floors. We were at the post office when I noticed one of the local vendors was selling mops! Ah, just what I needed. Lesson one, never get too excited about what anyone is selling. The price is dependent on the excitement of the buyer. Lesson two, know the price. I was speaking English, and so was he, but his amount and my amount were not the same. He said eight, but when he said eight, it did not sound like eight. You see, in Chichewa, the other national language of Malawi, no word ends in a consonant; every word ends with a vowel sound. The vowel he chose to place on the end of eight was an "I." So that eight now became eighty. I can understand eighty, so I paid eighty, and off he ran—fast. I looked behind me to see if an alien was about to attack because he simply took my money and was gone! The rest of the market seemed as calm as it did when I arrived, but that guy was still running for his life. I took my new mop to the car where a colleague, who was assisting us in our adjustment to this new place, met me. He said, "You bought a mop. Good for you," followed by the question, "How much did it cost you?"

"I paid eighty for it," I announced, "but the guy I bought it from just ran off." My friend began to roll with laughter. "What?" I asked.

He said, "He was asking eight for each mop. No word ends in a consonant. All words end in a vowel. You understood eighty and paid eighty. You made his day! You probably paid for his entire inventory." He could hardly speak through the tears of laughter. I was laughing too … on the inside.

You All Look Alike

It seems that no matter where we go, cross-culturally this is a common misconception: that everyone looks alike. We were on the campus of the Bible college for language learning, and when we finished our daily classwork in time, we could go to the chapel services with the students to listen as Chichewa was spoken. Often in these services, the students were called on to preach for practice.

It was also common for the missionary to be called on to pray during the service.

I admit, a few of my colleagues and I could be confused due to similar looks, dark hair, and glasses, and so to be called by their name and be expected to pray was understandable. But one time, I was really taken aback. Alicia and I had gone to chapel, and we were requested to sit in the front row. Things were going along nicely. The local pastor, whose congregation we had joined, was sitting next to me, and that made the service all the more enjoyable. The sermon was coming to a close, and the preacher for the day asked another colleague of mine, who I had not seen come in, to close the service in prayer. Now, you have to know that I am five foot seven on a good day. The colleague that was asked to pray is nearly six feet six, so I waited for his deep voice to begin leading us in prayer. After an uncomfortable lapse of time, my pastor gave me an elbow in the side and told me, "He's expecting you to pray." It is really hard to snicker and pray at the same time.

CHAPTER 6
Driving Stories

Roads

WE OFTEN JOKED WITH EACH other that the roughest part of any journey was our driveway. That was not always true. The road between the clinic and Salima became so badly eroded that it took as long to get from our house to Salima, twelve miles, as it did to travel from Salima to Lilongwe, seventy-two miles. During our time in Malawi, both of these sections of road were rebuilt. The section of road from our house to Salima was finished near Alicia's birthday the year before we left. Prior to the repairs being started, a large, I mean Large, perhaps **LARGE**, pothole developed in the road right in front of the clinic. If you were not watching the road and simply driving, and you happened to fall into this hole, you could do your car serious damage. A driver of a Mercedes Benz E series discovered this when he blew out both front tires and bent both front rims stranding himself and his family until assistance could arrive from Lilongwe.

It was also a bad idea to drive anywhere at night. Ox carts, goats, children, and broken-down vehicles are not required to have reflectors. We were visiting friends past dark when we made the drive home and had to yield right of way to the hippo. We also wanted to go find the local hippo pool we had heard about when we discovered the sun goes down more quickly than we expected. On that trip we were surprised by our one and only hyena sighting. Then there are always the adventures of getting stuck in the sand after dark trying to find hippos in unfamiliar territory. Accidents are often the result of those who believe driving at night should require no greater care than driving during the day. I cannot tell how many gave their lives by making this poor decision. Then there are the drivers: taxi drivers, who may or may not have a license, driving vehicles with limited braking systems and traveling the hills that separated Lilongwe and Salima; drunk drivers; overloaded vehicles; and pedestrian and animal traffic made driving any time hazardous.

It was fairly common for vehicle accidents to occur. In fact, hitting a pedestrian was also fairly common, even among the missionary community. I knew prayers for us were waning over the Fourth of July holiday 1995. I was staying at the Baptist guest house and driving to a meeting that was to be held at the Baptist Theological College. These two locations were on opposite sides of the Lilongwe River and thus across town as well. The road connecting the two was two lanes and often bumper-to-bumper as folks waited on the only two traffic lights to cycle. I was approaching the second of these traffic lights and could see I was the only vehicle not turning right. You know, of course, that in Britain and her colonies, other than America, people drive on the left side of the road from the right side of the car. So, I could see over everything turning right except the double-decker pink bus at the front of turn traffic. As I approached the light, called a *robot*, I noticed the people to my left, on the side of the street, making a great commotion, so I slowed. I was driving between twelve and twenty kilometers per hour—about eight to twelve miles per hour—when a man jumped in front of me carrying a stack of empty egg crates.

He hit the front of the van with a crash and was thrown to the middle of the intersection. Others from the side of the road collected his empty crates while others scooped him into the back of my van.

As we drove to the hospital, we were both very shaken. He spoke first. "God smiled on me today," were his only words.

I restrained the words screaming in my mind: "I don't want to be around you when God frowns." I left him in the hospital with a bruised hip that had hit the bull bar of the van and what had to be a pounding headache from the crashing of his head on my windshield, but he was still feeling blessed.

"Close By"

I don't know if it was a cultural thing or learned behavior to say whenever you are going to travel by car that a place is "close by" or "not far." I never really learned what that means, but I learned what it could mean. Prior to our moving down to the lake to assume our role as clinic administrator, the volunteer couple holding down the fort for us were asked if they would provide transport for a couple from the clinic. The dental orderly and his wife were expecting their first child, and she hoped to deliver closer to home so that family could be part of the joy. The volunteer couple assured the dental orderly of their glad assistance for transport, with the assurance that their home was close by.

The day came, and all loaded into the Toyota Hi Ace van for the *short* trip. It would have made sense for the expecting passenger to pack for the long stay at hospital and then the time at home, so the suitcases were not questioned. The van pulled away from the clinic and directions were given as needed. "How far?" was the frequently asked question, always with the response, "Not far." As the van neared Lilongwe, the capital city some seventy-five miles from the clinic, the question was asked again: "How far?" Now the response was changing: "Close now." When they were driving out of Lilongwe, the question came again, with the same response, and another hour later, the same response. As they neared Dedza, a small town an hour and a half away from Lilongwe, a turn was made off the main road with the assurance, "We are very close now!" Twelve miles later down the dusty, rocky, mountain road, the travelers had arrived! Over four hours of driving for the return trip still had to be made, but a definition of *close* was established.

You think I would learn from other's mistakes.

Now, before I tell this next story, let me just say it was expected that we do our part to employ local workers to do whatever they could. We had the resources; they needed the employment.

Our cook/house worker asked if we would take him to his village as one of his family members was ill. Just a side note: to receive the call that a family member is ill is the more polite way of saying someone in your family has died and you need to get home. I assured him I would provide the transport, and we made plans to leave early the next morning. We left at about six that Saturday morning from Lilongwe. We were still in language school at the time. I pulled into the village about three hundred miles northeast several hours later. I then retraced the roads back. The good news is, in Malawi, if you know the direction you are heading and you are on the paved road, you are not lost. You may not know where you are, but you are not lost. I drove over six hundred miles that day on Malawi's two-lane highway and returned home just after dark, glad his village was not far away.

You'd think I would learn.

Now That Makes Me Think of Weddings …

I had been asked if I would be a distinguished guest at another wedding. All I had to do was drive. The couple was from the youth group at Salima Baptist Church—the county seat church—and the same village. They had known each other for a very long time. I was told I would be driving the happy couple from the church to the village after the ceremony—a very short drive—and from the house of counseling to the reception—"an even shorter drive." That's in quotations because I didn't say it.

The day of the wedding came, and the groom and his party came dancing into church to the ever-affordable taped music. They gracefully stepped to their places as expected on the left side of the pastor. As the men were settled, the bride and her party began to dance in. This took an exceptional amount of time, and the altar was circled to lengthen the parade, but in time all were in their respective places. As this young couple was introduced as man and wife, the music started and they danced out to form a receiving line.

I, being the distinguished driver, opened the door for the happy couple, who soberly took their seats, and not a noise was made for the entire trip. I had the feeling someone had just done something wrong and they were waiting to get caught. We arrived at the counseling house: one for him and one for her. This is a time where the couple receives marriage counseling. We are accustomed to pre-marital counseling, but our ways are not for the entire world. This counseling session generally puts both the young people in shock. It certainly worked this time. The duration of the counseling was about two hours, and it was a pleasant enough wait. Then they emerged from their prospective mud huts, and we could proceed to the reception area.

I could see the house where the party was to take place! It was not more than a football field away! But could I get there? No! I had to drive with a group of women (the entire female population of the village) dancing, singing, and leading my way ever so slowly. It was very clear the elderly woman closest to my front bumper had been celebrating by drinking home brew for some time. You have to know there are very few automatic transmissions driven in Malawi, and none by missionaries. I had to keep the clutch in as we crawled toward the goal line. After forty-five minutes, my left leg was beyond fatigue; it had gone into all-out spasm. I was now nudging the inebriated, elderly woman with the car to avoid running over the entire mob. We did arrive, and no one really seemed upset with me rushing things along all that much. In fact, it was quite expected.

Upon arriving at the celebration, I was escorted to the hut of the distinguished guests. There I found the pastor, the reception's MC, and several of the church elders who had a role to play in the day's festivities. I saw they were already eating, so naturally, I joined in. Presently, a woman entered and made it exceptionally clear this was not *my* food, and I had no business eating now. My food was coming. All the men seated in the circle were taken aback by this display, and we sat in silence awaiting what I was to eat. It is a good thing they waited. African bow ties, Malawi sausages, were brought and placed still sizzling hot before me (African bow ties, that rare treat left for the very distinguished, are the intestines of the goat wrapped around themselves to resemble a bow tie). The pastor and other male guests looked at my meal in awe. After all, all they had was steak. When the woman who had previously scolded me left the hut, looks and lunches were exchanged. That was one of the best meals I had!

Driving in Wet Weather

I was often asked to visit some of the smaller churches in our district when I had a free Sunday. We generally only met with churches in associational meetings and not on a more casual basis. I had talked to one of the churches close to our *traditional authority's* house and scheduled a date to visit. That Sunday morning, we woke to a heavy rainfall, typical of the rainy season, but we had more free time in the rainy season due to farmer's schedules. We loaded into the car with our short-term missionary, who was working with us for a two-year stint as a school teacher for our older two children. She always tried to wear her lucky dress on Sundays. She felt that with this dress on, we were in for an adventure. I had a different name for what she called *adventures*. We headed over the wet, sandy road, trying to avoid the swampy areas and stay toward the dry sand. I passed the church, which was not unusual, so I had to turn around. I found a wider spot in the road, and again staying to the higher, drier sand, I turned. The car needed more room, so I was about to make my three-point turn when, as I gently shifted into reverse, the car sank. I don't mean the car started to sink; it sank! It settled at the running boards, and the suspension continued to allow the tires to settle deeper.

Our short-term mission colleague was thrilled. "What an adventure!" It is another long story, but I had a cell phone at the time, and I gave a friend a call. He knew exactly where I was and came in search. He found us, and as we hooked the vehicles together to pull mine out, I said, "Just keep moving." The sinkholes were everywhere. Some were mysteriously in elevated, dry ground, as I had found, and some were in the lower, water-filled pools. As my friend tightened the tow rope, he began to sink. He just floored his Land Rover, and my Prado came out of the bog. But that was not the only time I needed rescued.

On another occasion, I was driving home from a church during a light drizzle. I was just crawling along in four-wheel drive when I could no longer steer the car. I had drifted enough off center that I was sliding to the left side of the road. We were moving slowly—slow enough that the pedestrian on the left side of the road was moving faster than we were. It was a good thing too; she only turned around at the sound of the car coming to rest just inches behind her.

Then there was the driving to find the hippos and driving on the beach … where the thing just stuck.

Driving in Dry Weather

Driving in deep, dry sand is much like driving in snow. If the vehicle slows, you become stuck, and the vehicle can slip and slide. Our vehicle had not been handling well, but there was a drive that needed to be made. Alicia made the drive which was, as I recall, some distance away. The roads were still more potholed than not, and dodging the potholes was just a part of driving. The blessing was there could be no great speeds reached. Alicia pulled off the highway on to the road that accessed our house and had just reached the deep sand when the vehicle suddenly stopped. She walked the short distance home and informed me the vehicle was stuck in the sand just up the road. I went to make the inspection and found the left tie-rod had come undone. The sand was a mixed blessing. It stopped the vehicle, but it stopped it so quickly that the bolt to the tie-rod was directly under the car! I made the repair and drove home.

Another Ball

Alicia and I were headed to a church choir competition to be held at the marching ground of the nearby army base. We each were driving a separate vehicle. On my way in, I noticed the cadets playing a game of soccer in the field to the south of the road. One cadet kicked a ball way beyond the goal, and it landed in the road between our vehicles. Having no way to maneuver with a carload of passengers, Alicia ran over the ball. After the competition, Alicia's vehicle was mobbed by angry soldiers—a violent mob would be a better descriptor—wanting a replacement ball. The event really shocked Alicia, and three of these men were appointed to meet us at our house and get the money. Some things are simply unavoidable, but we did enjoy a peaceful relationship with the only group around that we knew had guns.

Tragedy and Humor

While driving in Malawi, we received our introduction to the local humor. Behavioral Violation Theory of Humor shows that humor has not evolved greatly in Malawi, where physical threats and violations of individual dignity create roars of laughter, even in their victims. Pedestrians, goats, chickens, nearly everything on the road it would seem, will try to cross the street in front of an oncoming vehicle. These close calls receive thunderous laughter. We learned that near-death experiences were a source of great humor. Unfortunately, they were also a source of great disaster as many people could not judge how quickly a vehicle was approaching versus how much time it would take to get out of its path. This tragic humor led to more than a few anecdotes that I'll enjoy sharing.

I had given piece work, a part-time job, to a young man who really had no capacity for work but wanted to prove himself nonetheless. I had asked him to cut some trees that were getting too close to the power lines that ran through the property. I had given him warning not to cut the trees too close to the power lines and leave those for someone with more experience. Well, the story would not be funny if he had listened. While returning home from my errands, I noticed a number of people running on the sandy road. I gently pulled alongside one of them and asked, "What is happening?"

I received the reply, "Fire!" Fire? I was heading to my house, and so were they! While not listening, this young man felled a tree, which hit the power lines, causing them to touch. This sent a blue flame streaming away in both directions, and when it reached the transformer, of course it exploded violently. The village had not had this kind of entertainment before. There was almost an air of celebration. I drove in through the gate and found the young man clinging to the saw and shaking uncontrollably. He was well enough, and no fire continued beyond the blue lightning bolt, but the laughter continued for hours, and whispers with snickers for weeks.

Malawians found humor not only in near misses, but in other's pain. When we arrived, our house would often flood during rains, as the footpath sloped toward the house. So when I gave instruction that our garden should slope away from the house and toward the lake to avoid flooding, I knew it was a large task. Our gardener, also Mr. Phiri (not related to our pastor or our language teacher; there are Phiris everywhere in Malawi) went to work, and the next day he came complaining of pain in his chest. We were initially concerned until he explained the pain. We provided some of that smelly ointment that relieves muscle pain but needs to be massaged in well. Alicia gave instruction to Mr. Manuel, our cook, to rub this into Mr. Phiri's chest muscles. We heard the row from inside the house, screaming, crying, and laughter. Mr. Phiri was writhing helplessly from under Mr. Manuel, who had him pinned under his knees, rubbing his sore pectoral muscles with great vigor, like bread dough.

Other's misfortune was always worthy of a good laugh. I was asked late one night to accompany a group of men from the church as they visited a sick friend at his house. I had the car, so we left from my house—not because it was far, but because we could arrive in style; that is taken seriously. Our sick friend was not the source of the humor, in case you're wondering. We arrived and had to park about fifty yards away. I was called to lead the group to the front steps of the house. There was a grass fence on our right to guide our way as there was no moonlight. I was told that when the fence made a sharp right to stay very close to the fence. When I asked why, I was told because there was a large sink hole to the left. I asked why, if they were more familiar with the area, it was I who was leading the way. Their reply was priceless: "It is because if you, white guy, fall in, we can see you, and we will know when to turn!" We did visit our friend, and as life turns out, years later he became the pharmacy clerk for the clinic.

Driving in the Game Park

We had several opportunities to visit Liwonde National Park in Malawi, and each time was an adventure. Visitors who assisted us in our mission meeting wanted to see the wild game of Africa and we were selected to be their guides as we had not seen much at the time either. The first adventure was getting lost along the way. The second was driving into the park for the first time and nearly dying from insecticide inhalation. Tsetse flies are known to carry disease, and mission vehicles at the time were not allowed to have air conditioning. This created a problem. We could either travel with windows up and die of the heat, or we could drive with the windows down and deal with the flies. A compromise was reached in consensus: we would drive with the windows down and roll them up whenever we stopped to watch the wildlife. During one of our brief stops, a fly was discovered in the van. One of our guests was determined to exterminate the fly with the insecticide spray. After filling the van with the choking mist, the label on the can was read and the warning that it must be sprayed in a well-ventilated area did not take us by surprise. The fly was released, and the windows stayed down the rest of the drive.

The same trip, we stopped on the side of the road because an elephant was spotted nearly four hundred yards off in the distance. "See the ears flapping," was the excited call. Being our first venture in, we had no idea that the reserve was not like a zoo, where you are guaranteed to see the animals up close. We drove into our camp and were taken on our boat safari. To be up-close and personal with the animals on the river provides a particular rush for the first-time viewer. Large crocodiles and one of the largest hippo populations in the world make the time on the river memorable. I was able to capture footage of one hippo chasing another into the river and the water exploding with the activity! I rewound the tape to make sure, and I shared the footage with others on the boat, only to lose it when I didn't go to the end of the tape to begin recording again. I think it was during the panic of seeing the lioness, which we were told was very rare. I began to film as the guide turned the boat, but by the time the boat was turned for me to get the shot, the lioness had vanished.

Our Second Visit

Both sets of parents came to visit us in Malawi, and mine were the first to come in April, 1996. We were to drive to the car park on the near side of the river and take the game-viewing boat to the camp, where we would spend the night after an evening game drive. The problem was, there was a huge mud bog just in front of the bridge we were to cross to get to the car park, and the drive around would take hours of daylight we did not have. Many from the village came to say they would help push us through the mud if we would pay, which begs the question how the road became wet in the first place. I was unwilling to pay, though the road was well rutted from a large truck that had just gone through. Mom just wanted to go home; she had seen enough for one day anyway. Dad and Alicia crossed the bridge on foot as I made plans to drive across. That's not to say they had any fear or had any question of my driving skill in the conditions provided. With no small amount of anxiety within the vehicle, I began to gain speed to hit the mud and avoid the deep trenches. Mud flying, engine revving, knuckles whitening, and villagers laughing, we avoided the river and arrived safely on the bridge! Once on the other side, we all took a deep breath and finished our short journey into the game reserve and to the car park.

Did I mention, I was lost again along the way? It may explain the time crunch, but it definitely explains the lack of fuel exiting the park the next day. But this was not the time to panic; I'd panic later and enjoy the time with family now. Once on the other side, we met fellow campers, who were later to become great friends, George and Susie. George was a guide and ran Safari Lodge outside of Lilongwe, a place we had been told about but never visited. George and I had mutual friends, and because of those ties, he was willing to provide me with the fuel I needed the next day to continue our journey. Crisis averted!

Our Third Visit

Our third visit came when Alicia's parents came to visit two months after mine had left. We drove into the camp from the other side, taking the longer but safer way around. The river safari provided the eventful moments of their visit. We set out for a relaxing ride. After visiting Mmvu Camp a few times, we could now really enjoy being among the wildlife. We viewed an extremely large herd of elephants off in the distance. As we drew closer, the exact size of the herd was discovered. Over sixty strong, it was the largest herd in Malawi! Our guide floated us ever closer: keep the visitors happy! Closer still! I could see the wrinkles in the trunks! Yet still closer! I was now seeing eyelashes! What does it mean when an elephant spreads its ears and shakes its head? I was in the front of the boat! I had great footage using my father-in-law's new video camera he had purchased for this trip. I did not even have to zoom to get a close-up view! In fact, I was wishing I could zoom out, and zoom out now, and zoom out fast! Yet our guide seemed quite calm as he explained when an elephant does these things, they are warning not to get too close. He then said they perform such acts if they are protecting their young, but as we saw no young at this time, our guide was rather confident in his skipper skills. This lead female charged just at that moment, revealing a previously unseen calf!

I was filming air, boat, water, and no amount of picture stability was going to fix the image. The guide was coaxing the small outboard to move faster, pull harder—anything to get us moving and now! I was nearly out the back of the boat before we started moving. I was just trying to get the nose of the boat out of the reeds to assist in our getaway; at least that would be my excuse! We had never been that close before, and we would never be that close again.

The Visit with My Brother-in-Law

Alicia's older brother came for a visit, and we drove the long way around again. This time, I didn't get lost! Figures, as you get to know a place. Again, you just never know what the reserve will hold as far as animal-spotting goes. We didn't see one elephant on that outing, the very thing that was desired. We always camped in an enclosure near the river's edge. Filming the hippos in the river in the early morning was magnificent. It was very still and peaceful, other than the noises of the hippos; they made sounds like very large pigs. I set the camera on the bank using the tripod, and suddenly a rustle in the foliage on the river bank under me nearly caused me to lose my footing. It was a large crocodile I had disturbed; I should have looked first. The next thing was the vervet monkeys that came to entertain us all and wake the resting. It made the disappointment of the lack of an elephant sighting fade a bit. After breakfast, we began our tedious drive out of the reserve.

Blesbok, antelope, gazelle, kudu, and sable were abundant, but still no elephants. And then, just off the rough, dusty road, there was a lone, young male elephant grazing in the acacia! We stopped the van just to take pictures, and to my surprise, my brother-in-law leaves the vehicle to get a better shot. It was one of those "you had to be there" moments. My brother-in-law moved so stealthily toward this elephant, with the breeze blowing his scent away from the animal's keen senses, that when he raised his camera to take the picture, just feet away, the motion caught the animal's attention and he raised his head, looking eye to eye with my brother-in-law! I don't know if it was a natural reaction on either's part, but instead of snapping that long, sought-after picture, my brother-in-law and the elephant turned at precisely the same moment away from each other and took flight! The sight created tearful laughter, which had to subside before we could continue our journey home.

Once back underway, we had not driven far when, my brother-in-law called out, "Snake." I saw snakes all the time. I was still looking out the window for elephants. At less than ten miles per hour, you could enjoy the world around you. His call did cause me to look forward, however, and see a log in the road. The log was moving! I never did get a clear view of that snake. With all the screaming, sliding of tires on gravel, and the gripping of the wheel, I was a bit distracted. I asked why he didn't say there was a snake. "I did," he answered.

I said, "No, you said, 'Snake.' You should have said, '*Snake!*'" All I know is that the road was twenty feet across and the snake

reached both sides at a diameter of a log. Its head was the size of a dinner plate.

That same visit, he proved that he was a fantastic uncle as he single-handedly captured a giant chameleon. The rest of my family was driving to the local resort for lunch when Alicia spotted the lizard. She asked her brother to get out and go capture it for the kids. There was some argument about chameleons biting and the desire not to be bitten. Assurances were given by the younger sister that these lizards do not bite. Hmmm, who knew? We named it Louie!

CHAPTER 7

More of Life

What Do You Mean No Joke?

THOUGH THERE WAS LAUGHTER, I discovered a terrible thing: there was no word for *joke* in my new culture. They did have a word for *jokester*, but no word for the story I wanted to tell. Those who know me know I love to have a good time and joke around. In fact, my high school graduation goal was "Chuck Barrett leaves high school to join Ringling Brothers and Barnum and Bailey to get paid for clowning around." So now there I was, fresh off the plane in this beautiful country. I was ready and eager to engage all who will teach me this language, except my wife. The more I learned, the more fun it was to get out and chat with people. God has a sense of humor. I wanted to tell funny stories as part of communication, but the stories themselves didn't translate either. So I had to begin with the introduction, "I want to tell you a story for the purpose of making you laugh." That just kills it, don't you think?

This time was known as "language torture" for good reason. You must acquire a small bit of a language you do not understand in a classroom where the only other student is your life partner, take that small bit out of the classroom into this new world around you, and somehow fit it into a conversation you do not know how to start. At

each opportunity, someone would ask, "Why can your wife speak better than you?" That would always make them laugh, but not me.

Look!

We arrived in Malawi in March, and on the Easter weekend, which seemed years later, we were asked if we would finally like to take the drive to the lake and see the place we would eventually call home— Salima, Malawi at last! We were more than excited. The drive, like all of them, seemed to take forever on winding, narrow, crowded roads. I had the sense of anticipation like awaiting Christmas. I couldn't wait to unveil the place we had set our sights on years earlier. We wondered, "How will we ever find our way around?" What we didn't realize at the time is, if you are on the paved road headed in the right direction, you are in the right place.

Somewhere along the terrors of the road, we slowed and pulled over. The mission colleagues who were driving us down to our future home had spent several years in the same station and were excited to show off the place they knew so well, the place where they had raised their own children. There in the distance was beautiful Lake Malawi reflecting the sun and stretching to both northern and southern horizons. We were enthralled. You know that dancing reflection of light on water? They have a word for that in Chichewa. The word *malavi* is very close to Malawi. I'll say nothing about imaginative names. I want to say—no, shout—"Hang on a minute. You have a word for 'reflecting sun on water,' but you don't have a word for 'joke'? You're kidding me, right?" Well, there it was, perhaps thirty miles ahead of us. We could have stayed and watched for hours, but within us was an itch to experience our destination. It seemed forever until we arrived. We left the paved road and turned onto a sandy path that led through the village. There were chain link fences and powerlines on one side of the road, and primitive mud huts on the other. This is the closest we had been to these dwellings up to that point.

About three hundred yards along the deep sand road, we turned into a property between two buildings. There were trees swaying in the breeze and buildings painted in blue and white. Here I'll have to interrupt my story. This blue and white paint was everywhere. All the buildings on this compound, and as I explored, all the buildings on the clinic compound were the same blue and white. It was a running joke in the mission regarding the price of paint that particular year. Anyway, we drove in, and up in the distance was the surf of the lake. We had arrived! The house was an older colonial style home, two stories tall with a wraparound veranda on both levels. Sometime in the past, the upper veranda had been closed in, which made the house seem even more monstrous. What you may or may not know is that 1994 was one of, if not, the coldest years on record. How cold? It snowed in Namibia! It was cold. The windows on the upper level veranda were louvers and could only slow a breeze, but did not seal. In a stiff breeze, they would add an additional whistle noise to the howl of the wind. I was not prepared for this cold. I was not prepared for the wind. I was not prepared for the sound of the surf. I saw the house, and although it was large, roomy, and wonderful, I saw a lot of maintenance awaiting my arrival.

We returned to Lilongwe to continue language learning, and a friend asked me, "How did you like the lake? Wasn't it wonderful?" He was surprised by my request for a transfer. It seemed so many people loved our house. It was famous as a missionary vacation destination, but no one wanted to deal with the clinic to live there. What can I say? I'm blessed. Sometimes I love sarcasm.

A Sight to Behold

We have seen amazing things. Over the years, one becomes immune to the sights and perhaps smells and sounds around them. For example, the beauty and splendor of the Rocky Mountains was never something we took for granted, but they no longer took our breath away as they did for visitors from other areas of our nation. The same can be said for the amazing things we saw in Malawi. These are just few:

On a regular basis, we saw women balancing huge and weighty bundles on their heads, leaving their hands free for other tasks as they walked distances. I remember seeing a woman balancing three one-hundred-pound bags of grain on her head as she stepped off the road. She momentarily lost her balance, and all that weight compressed her head onto her shoulder. Without a loss of stride, she somehow buckled her knees to get the weight back into proper position and carried on walking. Whatever needed to be carried—water, grain, tools, firewood, or shopping—regardless of weight or size, was handled in like manner.

We saw children standing of the side of the road with, what was that? We had to stop and find out. It was two sticks with mice stuck between them, looking very much like, well, a mouse kebab. They would find a hole, build a fire, and smoke the mice out of the back door to this mouse house. They would then boil the mice, dry them, and tie them between these two sticks to be sold on the side of the road. I never did try that mouse meat, but I'm told it is quite nice for the accurate nibbler. We have also seen children catching bugs and eating them. This could be fascinating, until it is your own child. Different people had their own delicacies, like fried grasshoppers, and different ways of preparing the familiar fish or termite dishes.

We have watched men making the most intricate carvings with primitive tools or fix flat tires with no tools at all. We watched mechanics under trees repair cars in ways that would confound their engineers. We were amazed watching people scratch a living where seemingly none could be found. At the same time, men sat idly by, playing games or drinking beer as the women over-worked.

We were stunned by animals running loose to be avoided by high-speed traffic, both domestic and wild. I had run over, but never killed, any chickens. I had to stop and wait for goats, cows, sheep, hippos, elephants, baboons, hyena, and giraffe. One evening we had to stop for a large hippo to cross the road after visiting friends. It was close enough to touch, so I rolled down my window. Alicia saw what I was doing and simply, quietly, and calmly requested I close the window as you never know how a wild animal will respond. I closed the window.

Termite mounds on the sides of the road, and really everywhere, seemed very much like grave markers in some places.

There were mud huts with thatched roofs in many different conditions: from well-painted and decorated, to dilapidated, to completely in ruins.

We even woke one morning at three o'clock to the sound of our German Shepherd/Rottweiler barking at a Fish Eagle screaming in the ebony tree in the front yard. Seems the eagle had dropped its fish, which had lodged in a branch of the tree just out of reach of the dog. Our dog also had encounters with baboons, water monitors (large lizards), snakes, and our other dogs. He even attacked and killed one of my prized goats, which was carrying twin kids.

The Big Dance

It would be a mistake if I did not mention "the big dance." This is part of African traditional religion, in which the spirit of the ancestors is kept alive by those who participate in this secret society. Men from the village will hide costumes in the cemeteries. Each costume has different significance and plays a different role within the life of the community. In our high-tech world, we might say, "We have an app for that." In this secret society, they have a mask for that. For instance, if a child misbehaves, the parents will not discipline him. A member of the secret society will don the discipline mask and deal with the issue. It is a great sight to see all the children running from the masked man as they all know have done something worthy of discipline. It takes years to learn all the masks and their function within society. There are hundreds, but it was always fascinating to see the men in costume walking along the road.

The Big Dance

CHAPTER 8

Getting to the Work

Yep, Five Years of Work

I REMEMBERED MY QUESTION TO Zeb Moss ("When I reach Malawi, will they pile five years of work on my desk?") as I reached the house in Senga Bay after language school. We had just moved in. In fact, the volunteer couple who came to watch over the clinic while we settled in was still on site. After a long day's work, I was greeted at the house by a carload of government employees. They were in my drive, awaiting my arrival. Why does it take five employees to do the work of one simple letter? I did not immediately start thinking about government misappropriation. The five Department of Labor employees seemed pleasant enough as they pressed their faces against our chain link fence, which looked over the lake. They turned toward me as I left my vehicle to make introductions. Their faces still had a blissful glow, which morphed as soon as we made eye contact—something like a predator that has just spotted its next target or those terrible childhood nightmares. They had come to tell me that I had a workman's compensation case pending against *me* from three years prior to my arrival (great news) and that if I did not clear this case, they would be back to arrest me in one week.

Yep, welcome to Malawi! There are always surprises in every new job, right?

Having no idea about the details of the case and a healthy fear of going into a Malawian prison, I went into high gear. I made an immediate request that the claim be paid. It was settled and paid in fairly short order, before the week deadline had passed. It was only after the claim was settled that I began to learn a cultural lesson: that critical information will often come too late to make a well-informed decision. I didn't go to jail, and I made a friend of the local labor officer ... not all bad.

Our House

We lived on a property that once housed the clinic, so it was a larger property with a large two-story colonial that we called home, a guest house, two workers' quarters, and the old clinic building. Maintenance was always an issue; there was always something that could, should, or needed to be done.

Just a Few Examples

We had a lightning strike near our house, causing us to experience some grounding problems within our wiring. We had a local electrician come and sort out these electrical problems for the most part, but the stove would still give a shock if you were barefoot. We asked what could be done to get this issue solved, and he told us that the lightning was still in the stove ... So, we just wore shoes.

Water

Our water supply was a constant issue. For the first several years, we had a submersible water pump and a pressurized tank that supplied the entire property. This worked well until a power outage, which always seemed to happen in the hottest season of the year. During those hot nights, you would feel each pore explode to try to keep your body temperature down. We called these hot nights by the number of times we had to wake up to stand under the cold shower to cool off enough to sleep. "It was a three-shower night" means it was bad. The ceiling fan did little to help cool us as it was blocked by the mosquito netting. I had malaria; I would rather suffer the heat than a bout of malaria. In time, we placed a large water tank on the old water tower, which we called fort Senga Bay. The new tank provided enough water to last a few days. It seemed that each year we would have to go down into the well and dig just a little deeper to keep the submersible pump below water. When we replaced the tank, we also replaced the pump, and we never had another issue. If the pump needed work, it was above ground, and repairs could be made in moments rather than days. What a great joy that was.

Power Outages

Power outages were seasonal, but not predictable. On one occasion, the power was out long enough for the freezer to thaw, ruining a good supply of meat. Well, not ruining … we had a massive BBQ and invited everyone for the feast. The extended power outages encouraged me to buy a generator. What did I know? Start the generator, plug it in, and off we go. Who knew that generators were so noisy and messy and needed to be tuned? I allowed the muffler to melt before I got a clue.

Bible School

I have said the property was large, and four families lived on the property most of the time, one being ours. The guesthouse was available except when we had a two-year missionary with us on station making that her home. One particular room in the old clinic building was nice and large, with a high step against the wall and sloping ceiling. I'm sure we could have used it for the home theater room if it were not for the heat and mosquitoes. It did make an ideal classroom, so when the Bible School was looking to decentralize, we had an excellent place in our district to house and school students two weeks at a time each quarter. It was also convenient as the teachers, our local pastor, the medical assistant, his wife, and I were closer to this location than any other. Just before departing Malawi, we were able to see nine of these men receive their Certificates of Completion for Bible School, which would allow them to pursue seminary if they desired or be recognized as a pastor within the local church.

I recall one evening as the students were gathered, the wind and rain were especially hard. When we awoke, we found tress uprooted and the dog run had been destroyed by fallen trees. I asked the men if they would assist in getting the fence repaired. "No," was the reply. "We are fearful of the dogs." I can understand and appreciate that. Duke, my Shepherd/Rottweiler mix, was particularly intimidating—a quality I thoroughly enjoyed. But Duke was just one of three dogs to be considered. I explained to the men that until the fence was repaired, the dogs would have free run. The trees were out of the way and the necessary repairs made within the hour.

CHAPTER 9
Old Clinic

In the old clinic part of the buildings, we made room for animals we raised in much of the space. We wanted turkeys for Thanksgiving, so we raised our own from chicks. We traded with our pastor: goats for turkey chicks. The goats were a fairly quick purchase when we arrived. We bought the goats to keep the vegetation under control, and they multiplied more rapidly than I expected. We also raised ducks and chickens, which made great pot pies but not much else.

We used one room to store and distribute grain for the World Food Program. We could secure the grain better and have it distributed without disturbing the operation of the clinic. Overall, the facilities proved very useful for many ministries.

There were times we had to deal with bees. We had four hives at one time, none of which were planned. One was in a pillar on our house; it was most difficult to get rid of, and I think Alicia has a picture of me dressed for battle. One hive was between the walls of the grain storage area, and I was asked by our employees if they could retrieve the honey. I made the stipulation that any damage to the building would need to be repaired, but they certainly could go honey hunting. What a wild battle: smoke, men dancing around beating themselves and the walls to get to the honey and remove the angry bees. But when the honey was gathered, there was great rejoicing. I was blessed the next morning with a jar of the harvested honey mixed with smoke and ash.

The Senga Bay Baptist Medical Clinic

Barrett family at Clinic

The clinic was on a separate property, about two miles away by car. On the opposite side of the street was the Malawi Armies Airborne division. The clinic included a very small waiting area, an examination room, a clerk's room, a dental room for exams (extractions mostly), two treatment rooms, a staff room, an air-conditioned pharmacy, an office, and a room where patients could convalesce for a few hours.

The clinic was started years before and then relocated to its current site, which was dedicated October 2, 1982, the same day I asked my beautiful friend, Alicia, to marry me. The great thing about the clinic was not the structure, though it provided a favorable venue, but the services and ministry it gave to the people. The staff would see an amazing number of children each month during our under five clinics and provide services to expectant mothers. When a cholera pandemic hit our area in 1998, the Baptist Medical Clinic, with no facilities to handle patients, had the highest survival rate of any health care facility in our district. We made a makeshift shelter from tarpaulins and privacy screens, and used the chain link fencing to hang the IV bags. I always appreciated the high level of service that was always expected from our clinic. We were known for having medication when the government hospital and clinics had none.

Knowing what we were charging and what would need to be charged to meet the goal of leaving a self-supporting facility left me with two options. I could either price the clinic out of the market by making it more cost -effective for the patient to take a taxi to the government hospital fifteen miles away, or build a private maternity clinic with a great reputation to generate the needed additional funds. I chose to build the maternity ward.

First, I needed a clear plan to present to the mission for approval. I had to have costs, plans, and pros and cons available to the mission for all to agree there was a need and that a maternity ward could fill that need. Through the support of two fellow missionaries, approval for the maternity clinic was provided. A neat maternity ward was planned and built. It provided a ten-bed main ward, with four private rooms with in-suite toilets and showers shared between two rooms. There was also a teaching area, two examination rooms, a delivery room that would allow for three deliveries, and a sluice and laundry room. It was dedicated in May 2002, and the major sponsors for the project were present at the ceremony. The Nurses and Midwives Counsel of Malawi was still not allowing us to open for some reason they could not really mention; perhaps because I would not bribe them.

With the maternity clinic built, the medical clinic would and could be self-supporting, and my task was nearly finished. I was ready to hand over the clinic to the Baptist Convention of Malawi, but I had no one to hand it over to. I thought my friend was looking forward to the responsibility, but he informed me he wanted to return to school instead to further his medical education. I was stuck. I called my supervisor and requested prayer for the matter.

We also asked the president of the Baptist Convention to pray with us. The next day, I woke with one name on my mind. I called my supervisor, who had exactly the same name! We then called the convention president, who too had the same name!

We contacted this person, who was the recently retired chief surgical nurse at the nation's largest hospital, and she was very willing! She arrived and began to serve, and noticed—how could you not?—the maternity ward was not in operation. She did an inspection and asked what the Nurses and Midwifes Counsel had said was still lacking. I told her I was unsure; they were just insistent it not open. She told me to schedule a date with them to do a physical inspection of the facility, and she would handle the rest. They came and did a walk-through, and I could tell they were very impressed, but still were hemming and hawing. I took them into our clinic staff room, which was set up for lunch and an ambush. Our new administrator was waiting in the staff room, and she was quite a surprise for those who had come for inspection, as she had trained the majority of nurses in the country in surgical nursing procedures. I was taking not a little delight in their surprise. She asked what they thought of our little clinic and why they were reluctant to have us open and start operating the maternity ward. They were dumbfounded and could only say they would give immediate approval. God is great. By God's grace, she was the right person in the right place at the right time!

Two weeks later, I was approached by her to ask if she could go home. *No!* I thought. *What have I done wrong?* She simply told me she had come from a funeral and had not gone home to pack anything. This was the only set of clothes she had. Could she please have permission to go home and pack to return? I gave her all the time she needed. When she returned, it took less than a week before things that I had been working to change for seven years changed under her watch almost overnight! I asked what she had done so differently to initiate the changes. She gave me a classic answer: "You just have to know how to talk to these people." I knew her words were no different than mine, but she could do what I could not. Again, God's hand.

Today the clinic is still going strong under the watchful eye of Mrs. Margaret Nyika. What a blessing. I can understand Paul when said, "I have not run in vain." But this is near the end of the Malawi story, and if it were really that easy, it would have been done without me.

CHAPTER 10

Leftovers Anyone?

WE LIVED IN SALIMA; AFTER all, that was our postal address. Salima was our district name and the name of the district town center twelve miles over rough road from our lakeshore home. However, we actually lived in the village of Mikhute (me koo' tay). But not just Mikhute, oh, no! We lived in Mikhute Two! That's the poorly made sequel to Mikhute. Seems the Mikhute boys could not get along. Mikhute, translates to "leftovers." Yep, that's right. We didn't even live in leftovers one! Nope, we lived in leftovers two!

I really cannot complain. Our house was on the shore of beautiful Lake Malawi! What a scene for eating meals. In the hot season, we could cool off with a swim! We could watch hippos pass by! Our house would have been buried in sand if we did nothing as the wind would blow a fresh layer of sand each day. We watched storms come across the lake from Mozambique. We ate and caught beautiful fresh fish. We listened to the surf day in and day out. Did I ever mention, I cannot stand the sound of the surf?

CHAPTER 11

Mentors

As we landed in Malawi, the FMB was starting a new mentorship program in which they assigned long-term missionaries in the field to those who were just beginning their service. We were assigned folks who lived in Mbeya, Tanzania, as our mentors, as they too had been assigned to a medical clinic. We were to visit their station first, and then they would come to see us in Salima. We made the plans, set dates, and secured our Tanzanian visa through the only legal means available, Tanzanian Air, though we planned on driving.

The drive was three days long. The first day we drove from Salima to M'zuzu in our mission-assigned Toyota Hi Ace van, which had seen better days and had aged rapidly with use on the unpaved sand or poorly maintained paved roads. It was older, had many miles, rattles, and drafts, but it ran and was reliable. The road from Salima North was a two-lane, winding, potholed, and, as all Malawi roads, unpredictable (because you could encounter animals, ox carts, pedestrians, or broken-down vehicles with no warning). We spent the night in the Baptist Guesthouse in M'zuzu and began our journey the next morning for the northern border of Malawi. We arrived in Karonga after driving down the escarpment, from which we had a panoramic view of Lake Malawi's northern end. We passed by Livingston, the mission station established by Doctor Henry Laws after failed attempts by the Scottish missionaries who followed the call of Dr. David Livingston to establish a place on the southern end of the lake. The area was beautiful, with native forest and blue monkeys providing adequate distractions.

Karonga, was the last town in Malawi before the Tanzanian boarder. We stopped at around four in the afternoon as the border would close before we could arrive. Our accommodation was a small motel type establishment on the shores of Lake Malawi. With dinner out of the way, the sun setting and no other form of entertainment, we settled into our room for the night. In no time we were disturbed by the sound of a large truck driving onto the compound filled with backpacking tourists. As the evening progressed, this group became more inebriated and louder. Our children slept through the raucous, but we remained vigilant until we knew they were settling down as well. I was so fatigued, I did not notice the cyclone that swept through the compound in the middle of the night. When we woke, we could see the aftermath of destruction as we made our way north to the border.

Once at the border, we were told our documents were fake and we would have to turn around and return home. I had paid good money for these fake documents, and I had come at great inconvenience. I was not about to turn around. The man at the border was clearly running a scam with the fellow we purchased the visas from in Lilongwe, so I asked to see his supervisor. It was not long before we had our passports stamped for clearance.

We arrived in Mbeya, a fairly typical eastern African city. The roads were nice enough if you were traveling through, but to go into the city or on any side streets, you would encounter potholes the size of most vehicles. The problem is you could not know the depth of the pothole as you entered, as they were filled with water. These potholes are the source of several amusing anecdotes and photographs. We guided our way, pre-GPS days, to our destination: the site of the old Baptist compound in the city.

Our hosts greeted us and made us feel welcomed, but there was business to attend to. The city had failed to provide adequate water to fill the cistern, especially with four visitors, to an adequate level to last a week; we needed to ascertain the reason. From the town's point of view, no additional water would be coming until the next scheduled fill day, as their system was inadequate to meet the demand. The neighbor's house on the compound had a full cistern, but the water pump was bad and needed replacing; or we could simply syphon water from one house to the other. Having worked in the construction and plumbing trades proved beneficial on the mission field; who would have guessed? We quickly went into the city looking for a replacement water pump, and we were fortunate to locate one. We were to learn, however slowly, that if you find what you need, buy it; it may not last if you shop around for a bargain. The tools and a helper were provided to me as I made the repairs. I disconnected the old pump and instructed the power be turned off, but there was a language barrier. Two hundred twenty volts surged through my body as I stood in the pool of water that had just drained from the loosened fittings. After sorting our communication problems, I proceeded to fit the new pump in place. We were ready to fill the elevated holding tank, from which we could syphon water to fill our host's cistern.

I was watching the small tank fill when a man walking below asked me a very personal question.

It seems the Swahili word for *work* and the Chichewa word for *wife* sound very similar. So, when this stranger on the ground asked about my wife, I was more than just a little curious. The helper assigned to me looked at the both of us and began to laugh uncontrollably. He translated for me, "He asked, 'How's the work?'" Well, after the electric and cultural shocks, the work was just fine. After five hours of pumping and syphoning, we had water in our host's cistern!

I don't know how to segue, but let's just say the stomach flu hit within two hours of filling the cistern. Who determines the adequate size of a cistern? The entire household, beginning with our son, caught that nasty bug, and we went through all that water in one night! Well, I'm glad the water was there.

Upon our return to Lilongwe, I looked up that fellow at Air Tanzania.

CHAPTER 12

Phone Service

WHEN WE ARRIVED IN MALAWI, we did have phone service, but the entire system from the switching station in Salima out was nearly destroyed by a lightning strike. There remained only four lines that went to the lake. Ours was not a priority, but it could become one for a price. During this time, I received a message from the local resort hotel that we had an urgent message to call home. Not having any clue as to what to expect, I sent Alicia with a guest and stayed home with her husband. In the lobby of the hotel, Alicia received the news her father had suffered a brain aneurism. This was a difficult time for us.

The guests with us were our mentors and fellow missionaries from Tanzania. So, now they were visiting us as we received this heart wrenching news. Neither of us ever traveled again to see the other, though it was advisable for the relationship.

CHAPTER 13

Church Life

My First Sermon in Malawi

I WAS ASKED ALMOST IMMEDIATELY upon arrival in Senga Bay when I would be preaching. Not being a preacher by calling, or training, or gifting, I was able to put the church off as long as possible. However, the days caught up with me, and I agreed to preach the first Sunday of the year in 1995. I believe I was doing well and was well prepared. Although I could not yet preach or understand a sermon in Chichewa, I could preach in English, and my friend and pastor could translate.

The morning finally came, and I was indeed nervous. As I sat, I noticed another white family came in and sat. I thought, *Well, at least they will understand me.* We came to a time in the service where we took up the offering, and Pastor called on this other white man to pray. The immediate thought came into my mind, *What? Could they possibly know each other?* This visitor prayed in unhindered Chichewa, and all the wind escaped my sails. I went to the front to stand beside my pastor as he introduced me, and as we started, it began to rain.

I don't know if you have ever been to the sub-tropics when rain begins to fall, but it begins as it finishes: abruptly. The church had a steep corrugated metal roof with no ceiling or insulation to baffle the noise, providing a hard surface from which it could echo. As I began to speak, I was shouting at the top of my voice, knowing the sound was not making it to the first row of people. Just as I closed in prayer, the rain stopped. I never have settled what I thought was going on: if I was not prepared, if the word I had prepared was not what God wanted to say to His people, or perhaps it was just for the pastor, who was the only one that heard it. Regardless, that was not my only time to prepare and not to be heard.

The First Baptismal Service I Conducted

Senga Bay Baptist Church is fortunate to be within a very comfortable walking distance to Lake Malawi, a beautiful setting for anything, but especially baptisms. The church allowed me to conduct this particular service as our oldest son, Barnabas, was one of the baptismal candidates. I had spent every free moment I had the weeks before learning and rehearsing exactly what needed to be said prior to baptizing each candidate. It was a language and cultural learning exercise and gave me some theological insights as well.

Sunday morning came, and it was just one of those perfect days: beautiful sun, light breeze, and a calm lake. I was so excited. I stepped into the lake and began to share how the water had nothing in it that gave it the power to save, but these people were coming to be baptized as a sign of their allegiance to Christ and to present a picture of His death, burial, and resurrection. I then moved out into the water to a depth from which I thought I could baptize comfortably and a distance from shore I believed could still be heard. I was greatly mistaken. (The first candidate approached, handing me a little slip of paper with his name on it. This always happened. The slips of paper did not come just because I was doing the baptizing. His name was Mr. Thousand, but I'll get back to that.) The water was too shallow, and I nearly broke my friend in half trying to get him submerged.

After my first failed attempt, I moved deeper into the water. I was now more than fifty yards from shore! I knew the crowd could no longer hear me, but the candidate could.

Barnabas walking out to be baptized in Lake Malawi.

I Baptized a Thousand

I could not wait to share this day with a dear friend! We drove to the capital, Lilongwe, and there, unexpectedly, was the one man with whom I had to share. I wanted to run to him, shouting, "I baptized a Thousand!" He met me, and before I could share my story, he said,

"We had a baptismal service yesterday, and I was able to baptize a Million! One of the guys gave me his slip of paper with the name Million on it, so I baptized Mr. Million." After hearing his story, all I could do was be glad for my friend. He always did have a better story, and together we found some good stories. Here's just one example:

The Power of the Cross

He and I were together at a conference and had a break and went walking. We came to a crowd on the road and stopped to see what was happening. In the center of the crowd was a traditional healer conducting a display of his art, hoping to drum up some business. We watched and stayed around after the show to have a chat with this man. He was interested in what we were doing and wanted us to see his place of business. He took us to a small mud hut with a thatched roof; in other words, it was a place that blended into the community. After our eyes adjusted to the darkness, we could see all his paraphernalia arranged around the room. He showed us the various animal parts, plant roots, and herbs, and explained each of their purposes. In the corner of the room, on a table off by itself, was a Bible, with a cross mounted on the wall above it.

The Bible and the cross seemed so out of place to us, and he did not speak to their use in his trade. We asked this man their significance for him, and he responded in excited amazement, "Do you know the power of the cross!?"

Easter Baptism

Being on the theme of baptisms, one story leads to another. We, P and E and my family, had been scheduled to go to Thonje (Cotton) Baptist Church for a baptismal service in October, but the day it was to take place, a funeral overruled our plans. The next time we could reschedule was Easter Sunday morning. We made the drive, only about thirty minutes on dry roads, and arrived. The church was a little concerned about the time, which was very unusual, but I didn't catch on. P asked if I were prepared to do the baptizing. I assured him I was, and he said, "Good. You baptize, and I'll preach." P likes to preach.

We followed the procession to the place they had prepared. Our son Zeb was still small, and he was carried by E, tied on her back as one of her own children would have been at that size. It looked to me as though a small stream, about a hand-breadth wide, had been blocked for days to make a pool large enough for the event. The water was very clear, and I checked out the pool before entering— you know, you never know. Frogs were making their home in this very clear pool, and as I stepped in, all five of them lined up shoulder to shoulder on the right-hand side of the pool as if for inspection. Cool. I entered, and we sang a chorus, and the first candidate came forward. You must keep in mind that a period of about six month had passed since the time we had scheduled the first service. More and more came, and a chorus was sung between each one, allowing me time to help them out of the pool, get the next candidate in, and read their name—yes, you got it—from the little slip of paper.

There were those candidates from different traditional backgrounds who wanted to be placed in the water three times, but by and large we were moving along quite well. There was the one young man who wanted to fall backward and have me take all his weight. Sad to say he discovered the one and only rock in an otherwise muddy embankment. He was fine; my hand was between his head and the rock. But folks just kept coming! P kept looking to see if I was tiring, but I did not understand his gaze. When all was done, seventy-eight individuals had been baptized that day. P then asked, "Isn't your arm tired?" It was not; I was ready for more! What a great day. Time was an issue. We still had to fulfil what was left of our task to preach, recognize all those baptized, dedicate babies, and eat. It was a good tired.

CHAPTER 14

Some of the Churches

Senga Bay

As I HAVE SAID, WE started our time at Senga Bay Baptist Church, which many in the district referred to as the Vatican. I'm not sure why that was; perhaps it was the pitch of the roof or perhaps because it was the *big* church in the district. It was because of this association, however, that the pastor of this church was referred to as the pope. Everyone thought that was funny too. I remember sitting in the congregation about two years into our first term of service, listening to the sermon and understanding what was being said! It was a major breakthrough! I realized what a great preacher our pastor was and made a point to tell him.

I was so wrapped up in the clinic, and my language skills were growing so increasingly, I felt as though more could be done. Previously, I would simply drive and transport the needed paraphernalia and personnel to associational training opportunities, but with my language getting to a level where I could hear, speak, and respond, I was given more opportunity to participate in teaching. It was during these weekend-long meetings that my language learning and cultural understanding would often take that ever-gradual step forward. It was during this time we became comfortable enough with our language skills to branch out from Senga Bay.

Ngolowindo and Charles Phiri

It didn't take long—perhaps it took too long—for Alicia and me both to reach the conclusion that we were not being used effectively just sitting in Senga Bay. The search for where we were to move was initiated.

The next Sunday we found ourselves in the Ngolowindo Baptist Church, only twelve kilometers along the paved road from Senga Bay to Salima and directly opposite the Islamic Training Center of Salima. The church leader was Charles Phiri. Charles was a seller of fish. Traveling from Salima to Senga Bay on his bicycle, he would buy a bucket of fish and sell them in the Salima market and then travel back again to Senga Bay for another bucketload if time permitted. He would never get rich, but he did provide for his family. Sundays would find Charles in Ngolowindo Baptist, providing spiritual leadership to a small congregation. We sat and watched, men on the left, ladies and children on the right—the men on mud benches while ladies and children sat on grass or bamboo mats on the floor. The strange thing was the mud pulpit at the front of the small building was the size of most old wooden pulpits you would expect in rural churches of America. Needless to say, it was unusually large and consumed a quarter of the usable inside space. Charles would transport his children and wife to church on the back of his bike and arrive about the time the Sunday school lesson would finish.

Choruses would be sung an offering taken, and Charles would preach. The crowd might grow to ten before the sermon. We began to attend and encourage Charles and the church in their walk with Jesus. We began to see growth as we worked and visited in the community. As my Chichewa improved, I would often get these small, crumpled pieces of paper handed to me, on which was written, "You are preaching today." Ngolowindo was where this started, and I quickly learned to have something prepared, but as I traveled more and more, these pieces of paper would reach me at nearly every church we visited. You learn to watch for the piece of paper being torn out of an exercise book, being rolled up tight, and then handed back. It's coming your way!

Ngolowindo Baptist Church

Then one Sunday after the service, a group of people came to us with a signed petition from the next small village up the road, Mackenzie.

Mackenzie and George Banda

Mackenzie carries the name of Dr. David Livingstone's son-in-law, demonstrating the rich history of Christian mission in the area. Now, over one hundred years later, the community wanted a church in their village, which consisted of less than twenty mud huts. The leader seemed to be our Sunday school teacher, George—more about George later. Charles and I had several discussions over the matter. The one that I recall the most was on the road as he was riding his bike and I was driving past. He flagged me down so we could chat. "If we start a new church, this great growth we have had (in Ngolowindo) will be cut in half," he protested. "I just don't think I can support this proposal." I had asked how many people were in the church just the year before and if the congregation was cut in half how many would be left, and Charles had to admit it was still growth.

Plans were then made, and a date was set for the launch service. May of 1997, the son of the missionary who began the work where my wife and I were serving came for a visit to his childhood home. He preached the sermon, the Senga Bay church pastor translated, and the entire community poured out to hear it. The next Sunday was to be the church's first worship, and all Ngolowindo's members had agreed to participate. Then the following week, each would meet separately, with George leading the Mackenzie congregation.

I can't remember where that next week took me, but I could not meet with either church during the first Sunday each was separate. I do remember that after that particular Sunday, I was driving to Salima when I saw Charles riding for his second trip to the lake. He flagged me down and told me I would never guess what had happened at the Ngolowindo church that Sunday. I was braced for the worst. Charles began to relate the story of how on that first Sunday the two churches met independently, two new families came to join Ngolowindo! His next statement has been etched in my memory and defines Charles: "When can we plant our next church?" Charles was one of nine men who completed their Bible School training while we were there, and he did well.

More about George Banda

George and I got along well, and when times were more difficult, I could find work for him to do to keep him busy until new employment opportunities presented themselves. My parents came to Malawi for a visit in 1996 and were honored to receive a chicken from our friend George. When our son Zebadiah was born, we traveled to South Africa for the birth. But not long after our return, George showed up the very special gift of a white rooster with black spots. From that time on, George was no longer known by his last name. In fact, I had to ask Alicia what his real name was, as I had called him Chicken George for so long.

George presenting chicken to Zebadiah

George also received training at our Bible school extension. We had received information that George and the Mackenzie church were both doing well. If you ever travel to Malawi, as you leave Lilongwe to the east, you will eventually arrive in Salima. As you are leaving town, you will find an Islamic training center on the right side of the road. Opposite the Islamic center, Ngolowindo Baptist Church stands just feet from the road. As you continue your journey, you will see a bridge. Before you cross, there is a village on the right-hand side of the road. This is Mackenzie.

Khapa Thenga

Once the Ngolowindo and Mackenzie churches were well established with leadership, and after we returned to Malawi for our second term, we again looked for a church in need of assistance. Khapa Thenga, as was mentioned previously, was at the major crossroad of the lakeshore highway and the east-west highway from Lilongwe to Salima. Khapa Thenga was a busy crossroad with high visibility. Prior to our getting involved in the church, I had attended the funeral of the previous church leader. It was here we had a wonderful team of volunteers from Oklahoma to assist in the reestablishment of this once-vibrant church. We showed the Jesus film, and the village poured out for the evening's entertainment.

Many lessons were learned here by all participants. I will say that cultural sensitivity needs to be vigilantly practiced by those presenting the Gospel to keep the doors of other's hearts open.

One Sunday, I was sitting, listening to the Sunday school lesson in Khapa Thenga, when I noticed a termite beginning to build a new hill out of the mud bench seat in front of me. As I watched, the mound and number of termites participating grew. By the time the lesson was over, the mound was four inches tall. Is it a wonder that termite mounds can grow to heights of over ten feet. Perhaps it was because of this distraction, but when it came time for me to preach, I began to speak of God being the owner of sin, which is not what I had wanted to say at all. Alicia, who was sitting in the rear of the building, simply said, "I don't think that is what you want to say." She was right. In Chichewa, the words for *sin* and *grace* were, for this learner, very close in pronunciation. We all had a good laugh, but I used the teachable moment to inform the congregation not to be shy in correcting what they know to be wrong, regardless of who is speaking.

Nangowo: My Idea or God's

On the road between Lilongwe—the capital city of Malawi—and Salima, there are many wide spots in the road where vendors gather to sell their produce. One in the Salima district particularly impressed me as a great place for a church. The area was known as Naluva, and it split the difference between Grass Baptist church, which was planted in 1994, and Khapa Thenga Baptist church. Being busy with the clinic and other church-related activities, I had limited time to pursue this venture. On a particular day, I discovered one of our church leaders also had a desire for a church to be established in this area. He was not exactly of the character of a church leader, but perhaps I was limiting God by being too American in my mindset. So, I placed my doubts aside to assist in making mud bricks and building this structure for the establishment of the new church.

Two side comments need to interrupt this train of thought for a moment. The first is about making bricks from a termite hill: termite hills make the strongest bricks because of the enzymes termites leave in the soil. The rigidity, though, makes the mound very difficult to break into useful dirt and not clods for making mud to place into molds. The second is that when termites are still in the mound, you need to work very quickly when mixing the water into the soil with bare feet or you will be bitten by the very active and now aggressive termites.

Barnabas mixing mud for bricks

With bricks molded, dried, baked, and ready, we set a few days aside for the construction project, and we all met bright and early. We had determined the size of the building based on the number of bricks we had, squared our lines, and began to lay foundation bricks. We had agreed that we could only go so high in one day to prevent the mud mortar from slumping under the weight of brick. We had an eager group of young people assisting us, and when we quit for the day, the young people must have thought it was because we were tired. We arrived the next day to find the walls to full height and badly bowed. The young men were very proud that they had continued to work after the old men gave up for the day. We slowly took the young men around the building, careful to thank them for the work, but pointing out exactly why we stopped. We showed them their great efforts would need to be torn down and another date scheduled to finish the construction as we again waited for the bricks to dry. We finished two weeks later, and the structure was ready for a roof.

God wastes nothing in our lives. I had worked construction on several types of buildings prior to college, and I knew a simple truss could be strong, affordable, and reproducible. I set out with our friend and gardener, Felix Phiri. I had shown him the plan, worked with him on how to make the plan fit any building width, made the first pattern truss, and left the men to the work. It was a long, hot day, but the trusses were up and ready for metal sheeting. We returned on another day to put the metal sheeting on the roof. It was another long day, but the building was finished, and you could see the gleaming new roof as you entered the valley from either direction!

We were told there would be a baptismal service there the following Sunday, preceded by revival services beginning Friday evening. We would not want to miss that. It was during this weekend that I wore new leather dress shoes, which I had never worn before. I arrived Friday and was told as we met as church leaders and pastors that we would have to walk some distance to the river for the baptisms and the river may not be deep enough. I thought it would be a good idea for us all to check the river situation prior to Sunday to avoid disappointment. When folks who are used to walking tell you it is some distance away, take notice. We all agreed and walked at a brisk pace. It took forty-five minutes to get to the river. My feet, in the new leather shoes, were blistered and in great pain; then we still had to make the trek back. The river would indeed be adequate. Well, of course it would be, silly missionary. Sunday morning came and I know I walked at least some distance barefoot, but we had a remarkable, unforgettable baptismal service. It was unforgettable due to the fact that for the first time in my life I watched four men deployed just to serve as crocodile alerts as the pastor and baptismal candidates entered the river.

Our work with other congregations kept us from Naluva for some time, but as we had opportunity, we would return. Time after time, we found the building empty. Why after all the work, the vision, the passion, would the building be empty? I knew that at some time in the construction process, the church leader who had the vision for a place of worship here had abandoned the people, but I knew nothing of the cause. Finally, a friend came and said, "The people don't live here. This is just a place they come to sell their produce." He later took me back into the place where the people lived, Nangowo, which I discovered was also the home of his wife's family. We spent several months back in that area under the baobab trees without a building, developing a new group of worshipers. It was not the place I had chosen, but I was able to see God at work in this village off the road, bringing people to Himself under the baobab trees.

In time, this small but growing congregation needed to hold its own baptismal service. My friend and I, along with his family, went down to the river, which was much closer, and baptized those wanting to identify themselves as Jesus's followers. One old man especially comes to mind. His name was George Maseko, though I'm sure he has gone home to be with his Lord by now. George was old and had arthritis in his knees to the point he could not walk without a cane in each hand during the warmer weather. In the cooler weather, he needed the assistance of a wheelchair. We gathered for baptism and discovered the bank to the river was longer and steeper than we thought. Getting George down was the problem. Four of the small congregation gathered around him, much like the paralytic was brought to Jesus by four friends, and lowered him to the river. In the cold water of the Lilongwe River, George was baptized with great rejoicing!

I would not have chosen the baobab trees, even if I could have found them. I chose the prominent sight on the side of the highway. I found God wants me to join Him in His work getting to people, not trying to drag people to something I want to create for Him. God's plans are a great deal more fun, adventurous, and rewarding!

We had to cross a bridge to get to these baobab trees. It was a bit nerve-racking at first, but we discovered it was very strong. We encountered a huge baboon on this bridge while going to church one morning. When I say huge, I mean it was gargantuan. It was also here that our son, Barnabas, taught his first Sunday school lesson. It was here our vehicle slid into the deep drainage ditch graded into the road but was pushed out by many men of the area. Few things build relationships with people like needing their assistance. In fact, a genuine "How can you help me?" places the person you are talking to in a position of power, and in sub-Saharan Africa, this will get you farther down the relationship trail more quickly than remaining calm, cool, and collected.

CHAPTER 15

Some of the People We Met

I THINK IT MOST APPROPRIATE to begin my *people* stories with the story that brought Nigel and I closer as friends. I had known Nigel for some time. He was a younger man who lived just a few miles south on the lake. He was a mechanic and Thames riverboat skipper, the son of parents who decided to make Malawi home after their stint in serving Britain. Barry is Nigel's father. Barry was working to make a beautiful marina out of what was once a cannery operation on Lake Malawi. I don't want to interrupt this story, but I met the man who built the cannery years later in South Africa! Anyway, Barry and Nigel had helped me with a boat I'll tell you about later by providing me a place to work. They also assisted with other small engine repairs on other equipment. Barry pulled me into his office after one short visit and asked about a matter regarding his health. Even now, my heart is moved by these events. I told him I would get back to him, which I did the next day with the news he already instinctively knew. He had neurological problems, and after doctor's visits, it was determined he needed to return to the U.K. for treatment.

Barry was away for nearly a year, but upon his return, he was just the shadow of the man he was when he left. He had been diagnosed with brain cancer and wanted to return to his beloved Malawi as his last resting place. He passed away not long after, and I received the call from Nigel of his passing. I assisted in the arrangements of Barry's last wishes to be cremated and have his remains scattered on the lake.

None of these details bring great memories to mind, but they allowed Nigel and I to share in a time of grief and that always binds the hearts of people together. I know I could have eulogized Barry so much better. I was proud to be, even just for a short time, his "pastor-friend."

The Boat (*The Good News*) and Auntie

I will tell you other stories as they intertwine, but it necessitates not telling chronological stories.

Alicia had shared with me a number of times her feelings of being trapped at the house while I was off with the car. Paradise is great if you can enjoy it. It is difficult to take advantage of the lake through swimming and other water sports and keep a proper image among the rural populace. You see, if a woman wore even shorts in public, she was considered to be for hire. So, if Alicia were to enjoy water recreation, it would have to be at the local resort hotel's swimming pool. But this required a means of transportation. I once said, "It is just down the road." I really believed that until we took that walk as a family, nearly one hour. Just down the road indeed.

So when an opportunity was presented to purchase a boat, we didn't think twice … perhaps not at all and made the purchase. They say the happiest two days of a man's life are the day he buys a boat and the day he sells it. This particular vessel was seventeen and a half feet long and looked like something from a Sean Connery-era James Bond movie. Well, we were pleased to be able to have a means of escape. The boat was taken out on occasion, with disappointing results. Its failure to start was the most frequent of disappointments. But there were others as well.

Once Alicia took the boat out to the resort hotel, and as she and the children decided to return, the boat would not start for her. She asked a scuba instructor friend for assistance, and as he jumped into the boat, he went through the boat's decking, but it started. I made repairs. We left Malawi in a hurry in 1997 (another story), so I left the boat moored. Upon returning to Malawi, the boat had two holes worn in the hull from the rocks as the lake levels dropped during the dry season. Again, I made repairs.

This time I was serious! With the help of Nigel, I ripped out the subflooring, replacing it with new hardwood, new decking, and new fiberglass over the damaged exterior areas. I cut out the fiberglass top in the front and dropped it to make a bow seating area. I repainted this old craft to look like the new beauty she was becoming. I decided in the rebuild that she needed a name. Already on the lake there were boats named *Bad News* and *No News*, both belonging to the same family, so naturally, being the missionary and preaching the Good News, it seemed appropriate for the *Good News* to haul us across the water! I built a bench in the back for seating and storage. I must be a bit of a red neck as I found reclining bucket seats that I mounted for the pilot and copilot. This was now looking good, but I did not get a chance to finish what I started. I really took care with this project and wanted my family to enjoy the opportunities the boat would afford.

All this to get to Auntie. We were still looking for the proper vehicle for Alicia. On a trip to Lilongwe, I found an advert on the window of a gas station with a car for sale, and I just had to take it home to show Alicia. This was a beautiful 1972 Rover 2000. It was gorgeous, with rough and aged leather seats, but with only fifty-three thousand miles! I showed Alicia the picture, and she was instantly taken with the car. I made a call to my friend Nigel, who was a great help. Nigel's mechanical training was specifically on these older British classic vehicles. I asked if he would mind making a trip to Lilongwe with us to check out this car. A date was set, and we met the owners in the parking lot of a shopping center. We checked the car out—mostly Nigel and I—and after a thorough inspection, he said, "If you don't buy this car, I will." The couple selling the vehicle nicknamed the car "Auntie." They said it was because she was just such a gentle, charming old gal. They were Scottish, as if that matters. We bought Auntie.

We enjoyed the way it looked and drove. It was an Alicia car, and she looked stunning in it. We purchased the car in April and had no real call to drive it much until June, assisting friends with wedding reception arrangements. After the wedding reception, Alicia commented on how the car was not shifting as it should. I called Nigel. He said he would be over sometime to collect it and take it to his shop at the marina, where he had the tools and room to work. Great; no problem. Nigel came, collected Auntie, and took her the six miles back to his shop.

Now the nearest place to take care of anything was Salima, about twelve miles away from the lakeshore. It is fairly flat, and you can see for miles. I made this trip regularly, as shopping, banking, paying bills, and making postal runs were part of everyday life. As I was returning from town about lunchtime, I saw a plume of smoke rising in the southeast. It was worth notice, but not totally unusual. I returned home and could hear the phone ringing. The new lines had been installed just months before, I heard Alicia answer, and as I came through the door, she said, "It's for you. It's Nigel."

"Hello," I said in my usually chipper voice.

"Chuck," he said with hesitance. I already knew. "There has been an accident at the shop, and your car has burned"

"How bad is it?" I asked.

"No," he said. "Your car has *burned!*" Perhaps louder English would get his message across. "All right, I'll meet you at the marina." I left immediately. I arrived to find a very distraught Nigel making apologies for the accident, but he was not there at the time of the incident, and there was nothing he could do. His employees, seeing the fire, towed the flaming vehicle outside the shop and extinguished the fire with sand. As I inspected, Nigel's apologies were unceasing. I assured him it was not a problem. My wife is still the proud owner of a piece of charcoal in the vague shape of a Rover 2000 somewhere in Malawi. Friendship is to be valued higher than the most expensive car.

As we made the move from Malawi to South Africa, the boat had no place in our future. It had to go. A colleague and friend from Mozambique purchased the boat, and on his journey, the shock absorbers of the heavy-duty trailer were forced through the bottom of the boat. He made repairs.

Gordon Wilson

Melanie, Gordon's daughter, was a young lady who came to the lake to work at the local beach resort hotel. We all—Alicia and I, Thomas, Melanie, Nigel, and the young teacher the hotel owners had brought from their home country to teach their two children (the same ages as our older two children)—made quite the social club. To shorten a long story, Thomas and Melanie fell in love and wanted me to perform the wedding ceremony. A date was set, plans were made, the family came (even my parents), and we celebrated the engagement. The wedding was beautiful, though the day was *hot*. Thomas was not perspiring but raining. We were all in suits and miserable, but looking forward to the joy of the day. From the time Melanie walked through the back door, escorted by her father, Gordon, to the time she walked out escorted by her husband, Thomas, it was a total of fifteen minutes of sweet tears and sweat. I was later toasted by Gordon at the reception for having such a short ceremony.

Chuck with Thomas and Melanie Wendel

Now, you know Gordon. We enjoyed moments, regardless how brief, as I was the only pastor he knew. Gordon was later diagnosed with cancer and unexpectedly survived a surgery. He flew to Malawi and wanted to see me. Well, I was ready and had my sermon ready. I was going to answer his questions and bring him to Jesus. When he arrived at my house, we made him comfy and had a table ready outside for our chat. He wanted to talk about his wife and asked that I pray for her. That was it: no questions, no further seeking on his part. It was there he shared with me that I was the only pastor he had ever known. After just a brief time, he left.

Gordon lived in a suburb of Johannesburg, South Africa, which is a long way from the shores of Lake Malawi. We received news he had gone back into the hospital and was not expected to live. He did! This was just a few weeks after Auntie had burned. I went to Alicia and said, "We just spent fifteen hundred dollars on something that did not last. I think I can spend four hundred and go visit Gordon and perhaps invest in eternity." Alicia agreed. We bought the ticket, and I flew down to Johannesburg.

We had already made great friends in Johannesburg, as we spent two months there preparing for the birth of our youngest child. I coordinated with my friend to get me from the airport and schedule a meeting with Gordon. Prior to leaving Malawi, however, Melanie had some specific instructions for me. "Make sure Gordon's wife, is out of the room prior to talking to him. She has had nothing nice to say about Christians and may stop you talking with Dad."

So, off I went on my merry way. My dear friend met me at the airport. I called Gordon to schedule a visit, and he gave me his address. When the scheduled visit came, my friend drove and went in with me as we visited with Gordon. His wife never left the room and made it clear she had no intention of leaving while I spoke with him. As I began to share with Gordon about what I believe and why (the Gospel of Jesus), I noticed his wife paying particular attention. When I finished, I asked if Gordon would like to receive God's forgiveness offered through faith in Jesus's redemptive work on the cross. He said yes, and so did his wife! Why do we get shocked when God does His work so well? I made sure before I left that there was a Bible in the home, and assured them of my continued prayer for them. I made sure they and my friend were able to contact each other.

When I arrived back at my room in Johannesburg, Melanie called asking for a report. I informed her that her father and step-mother had both professed Jesus Christ as Lord and expressed their desire to follow Him! She was stunned. She said she was flying down to meet me. In my mind, what really happened was she bought a ticket just to meet me at the airport and fly back to Malawi with me so we had uninterrupted time for me to tell the story. She wanted to hear it again and again.

I suppose that is how the story of Jesus should be: always fresh.

Now on to some others

Anderson Chigala

Anderson Chigala had one of those life-changing testimonies that impacted many of the people around him. Anderson liked to drink. He also liked to get married. He simply had a difficult time staying both sober and married. In fact, Anderson was known as the village drunk. His village, Namwera, was one of the six places our Baptist Medical Clinic held mobile clinics. When Anderson was confronted with the Gospel of Jesus Christ, it so changed his life that the folks in the village really paid notice. "What happened to you?" they would ask, and he would begin to share his story. His testimony had such an impact on the place where he lived that many came to Christ. So many, in fact, that a church was erected near the highway. A church had already been established at the site of the outreach clinic some two miles east.

As time went by, people would move from that place to another and miss the body of Christ in their new location. They would call Anderson to assist them by having him share his story of how he came to Christ in their new place, and again, many people would come to faith in Jesus. This happened over and over, and at the time of his death, seven churches could directly tie their beginning to the testimony and evangelistic work of Mr. Anderson Chigala.

I told you the original church was built beside the highway. It was built at a curve in the highway, only twenty yards to the east. The story you hear about what happened to that building really depends on who you talk to: either a car or a large truck tire left the road and crashed into the church building. Either way, the building was destroyed, and a new building had to be built. The old church site was where the cemetery had already been established prior to the move. The new church was well off the highway, three hundred yards off the highway to the west, to prevent a recurrence.

We had received word of Anderson's passing and made plans to get to his house. We were met by a large crowd and a very prominent member of the Baptist Convention of Malawi. It was then I heard the complete story of the man I had only met a few times in my travels. The sermon at the house was delivered, and we made our way across the highway to the cemetery. There was, as is tradition, another sermon delivered before the lowering of the casket. As I stood there between friends, I made an observation. I told P, standing to my right, that they really worked hard to dig Anderson's grave because they had to dig through a layer of bricks. P made mention to the pastor of pastors, standing to my left, and the two became still and quiet. I knew I was missing something, so I asked. P replied, "Don't you see where you are?" I was in the middle of a cemetery. I knew where I was, but as I stood and gazed at the scene, I noticed the exposed floor of the old original church building. P then said, "Those bricks are at the threshold of the original church building Anderson helped establish and build." The moment immediately took on significantly more meaning. The plot had not been reserved; they were simply digging the next plot over from the last grave. Yet there at the threshold, they laid the town drunk through whose testimony many came to faith in Jesus; and this ruin of a building was the first representative church, started as a result of his sharing. We agreed, as we watched in awe, that Anderson would have been honored.

P and E

I really want to introduce you to my very dear friends, P and his wife, E. P was, and is, a rare individual, trained as both a medical professional and theologian. P always had an opinion and was rarely hesitant to speak. It was all well and fine with me; I had much to learn, and he had much to share. Over the years the clinic was in operation, several small churches were established as a result of the clinic's outreach efforts. In fact, nearly all of the thirty-two churches in the Salima district at the time could link their beginnings with the clinic directly as the result of an outreach clinic, as a generational plant, or indirectly, where the administrator or other clinic-tied personnel had a hand in starting the church. P was, for the most part, the clinic's chief medical assistant. For the other part, he was away getting further education in one of his two fields of service. When P was at the clinic, he and I were never wanting for something to do. There were always churches asking for training or the ordinances.

Regardless, P and I were nearly always together, a fact that was both a comfort and agitation for our wives.

E, P's wife, was also a rarity. E had been seminary trained to assist and teach many of our ladies in church what it meant to be a disciple of Jesus. Unless you have been in this situation, it seems strange. Men teach men and women teach women. Men and women even sat on different sides of the building during services. There was a need for female deacons to minister to the women. Otherwise, the church leader would either compromise himself and the woman to whom he wanted to minister, or the woman would never receive ministry. Anyway, throughout our time, E was a great blessing.

I recall one particular meeting we were scheduled to hold on the southern edge of the Salima district over a weekend. Both P and E were suffering with malaria but on the mend, and we hated to reschedule meetings as the schedule was so tight. We could not get away earlier due to P needing to finish some clinic work with a patient. "Sickness knows no time," was always used when other schedules had to be interrupted. By the time we did get away and make the drive to the appointed location, rain had fallen and the river was flowing over the road, cutting off access to the area. We stopped at the closest church that would have been a part of that meeting, because the sun was setting and it is never a good idea to drive at night in Malawi. We struggled to make ourselves comfortable in the vehicle, swatting mosquitoes and avoiding rolling down windows to allow others in, as no place was prepared for our unexpected arrival. You see, when you go to these meetings, it is not to sleep; it is to teach all through the night.

Now, no story happens in a vacuum. Related stories impact what is going on around you all the time. At this particular time, we were dealing with an issue regarding a Baptist missionary—not related to me, any of my colleagues, or our organization in any way—who had shot and killed a man earlier in the year. So, here we are: I've given P and E the front seats, which recline and can make for less of a great inconvenience, while I chose the rear of the vehicle, which is already full of books and supplies for the meeting not taking place. We were about to find the least uncomfortable position for sleeping when there was a knock at the glass, which startled us all.

We were told our meal was ready. It was now late. Why disturb us at this hour? The reason: "We were afraid that Mr. Barrett (being a Baptist missionary) had a gun, and if we disturbed him, he may shoot us." P used this teachable moment to assure them I had no gun and would never harm to anyone if I did. Oh, yes, two weeks later, the incubation period for malaria, I too came down with it. We all knew when and where it occurred.

A Later Date

After our rained-out meeting, another was scheduled, and we made it to Pastor E's place. Flat and sandy with cassava growing to green the landscape, which was eerily dotted with leafless baobab trees (those that look as though they had been planted upside down), Pastor E's small village did not appeal to many, and very few made it their home. Due to Pastor E's face shape, he always had a smile on his face, whether he was angry or laughing uncontrollably. In the course of the meeting, someone asked me my opinion, but before I could answer, Pastor E chimed in. "You can't ask him. He doesn't count; he's harmless." Regardless if he was angry or not, the grin spread across his face. I began to laugh, which relieved the tension in the room, and we all began to laugh. What a great time that was.

Zebadiah

We have served with some very dear colleagues over the years, and I was always curious about their families. One family served as agricultural missionaries in Malawi and had three children and loved our children effortlessly. This family never had electricity hooked up to their home, but rather powered up the generator for a short time every evening prior to retiring. This family had three children, the youngest of which was several years younger than his siblings. The wife of this dear couple just said in a casual conversation, "You know, had I known what a blessing children are, I would have had more of them." I took this to heart and began discussions with Alicia over the statement.

Another couple who came to the mission had left two children in the States and brought two younger children with them. We thought this was a beautiful arrangement, and Alicia and I looked on this family with amazement. How great, we thought, such an arrangement must be. They too were an inspiration to us and encouraged us to have more children.

Alicia and I had two precious, beautiful children, but we had always wanted four. Timing was difficult as were Alicia's two previous deliveries. It was not long before we agreed to start a "second family" so to speak. Alicia had always said she did not want to be pregnant in the summer months, as she struggles with the heat under normal conditions and pregnancy would simply multiply the misery. June through August are the cooler months in Malawi, so we planned for a birth during that time frame.

Well, everything was normal up to the time of delivery. I was very involved in the medical field in Malawi, and I was sure I did not want Alicia, with her past, delivering a baby there. Arrangements were made, and we traveled to Johannesburg, South Africa, a month prior to her due date, as the airlines allowed. We spent about two months there in Johannesburg: one month prior to and one month after Zeb's birth. In that time, we made great new friends and met several doctors who would be important to our journey later on.

How did we come to the name Zeb? Well, in the womb, this new life was proving very strong, so we wanted to choose a biblical name that meant "strength." Unfortunately, we knew children with those names, and it is always difficult to give your child the name of other children around them. So, we changed focus to "gift of God," and we found Zebadiah!

The Story within the Story

Years before, when we were called to missions, we came into contact with Zeb Moss, a missionary who had served years in Zambia. When Alicia had called our mission agency's office, Zeb was the missionary who answered her questions and placed a sticky note on our file that simply said, "Chuck and Alicia Barrett—good match." Four years later, we were in Malawi. So, we came to "gift of God," and had a great experience with the only Zeb we had ever known, and the Zebadiah we encountered in scripture was a missionary (priest) for King Jehoshaphat (2 Chronicles 17:8), so Zeb's name was settled. Our oldest son is Barnabas—go figure.

Now, in Johannesburg awaiting the birth of our third child, we really had no worries except that the hospital was in an area of the city that was not the greatest. Labor finally came, and we made the trip. Like all couples, we had questions: Will he be healthy? Will he be normal? Will all go well? I was able to be with Alicia until the labor pains became intense enough for her to receive her epidural. Suddenly, the labor room became alive with activity surrounding my wife. I stopped one young intern and asked what the problem was. "We are looking for an epidural needle!" he explained. I was floored.

"I came to Johannesburg to avoid problems such as these. If I would have known you needed an epidural needle, I would have brought you an epidural needle!" I said in an extremely calm voice.

My wife not only received some pain relief, but also some spinal nerve damage, which did not subside for years. The experience left us fearful of another delivery. The damage done could be reinjured, causing permanent spinal damage and paralysis. We just knew that child number four would never come.

Zephaniah

Zephaniah entered our life one morning as a family across the sand road in our village discovered the discarded baby delivered during the night by their daughter in the family's pit latrine. The baby's grandmother heard whimpering in the sewage of the latrine and quickly had others begin digging to retrieve the baby. He was brought to the surface and immediately taken to the clinic, and we were called. Our friend, P, the medical assistant, told us the heart-breaking story and said there may be no one to take care of the child. The baby was cleaned, inspected, and given his newborn injections. The grandmother was told he needed to be under constant surveillance to insure that infection would not set in. Since the mother dumped the baby and left the village, he would need nourishment, which is why we were called.

Requests were sent out and responses were received, and we began to provide powdered milk and formula for the baby. There was another problem: the baby had no name. The medical assistant who had cleaned the baby gave Alicia the task of naming him. She decided on Zephaniah: "protected by God" or "God is my protection." I believe that was appropriate. We were able to watch Zephaniah for a few years as he grew. His grandmother insisted he was her baby and would not think of allowing another family to raise him. He was just younger than Zeb, and the jury was still out as to Alicia's pain and condition. We could decide to have another if her pain was to subside in a reasonable time. Zephaniah was a beautiful baby, and the grandmother needed so much assistance to understand how formula worked and just in watching out after him that the medical assistant made constant inquiries into whether the grandmother would not rather have someone else raise him. The question was always answered in the negative.

We often think about Zephaniah on October 1 and wonder, now that we are removed, how he may be.

Pastor Testament

Not far from Pastor E's place, there is a turnoff where you can buy wonderful, large carvings from artists trained at the nearby Mua Catholic Mission, which celebrated one hundred years of service while we were there. Pastor Testament was a young man with a burden in that particular place because of the large population of Ngoni, descendants of the Zulus. Pastor Testament was very quick in planting and establishing what I liked to call Mua Catholic Mission Baptist Church. Pastor Testament would come by from time to time for advice, prayer, encouragement, and to schedule training meetings in his area. I was able to watch him mature in his walk of faith and manhood. We worked together as the congregation grew and a building was built. We had more than just a missionary-local pastor relationship; we were friends.

Alicia and I were able to attend his wedding, and when his son was born, I traveled to his home for the celebration. I could not help finding humor in the situation and shared with him my amusement. There was before me the old Testament holding the new Testament. I have the picture.

Chuck with the Testament family

CHAPTER 16
Just Stories

What to Wear

In Malawi, I often wore a pullover cotton shirt that was tie-dyed and embroidered. The shirts were cool in the heat of Malawi and acceptable apparel for the church setting. P, on the other hand, liked to dress in a suit and tie. We were often called upon to travel together to churches that had no pastor. At the best of times while I was in Malawi, the thirty-two churches in the Salima district had five trained leaders. We were called this particular Sunday to Mwala wa Mtanda (Rock of the Cross) Baptist Church. If you approached the rock just right, you could make out the shape of the cross. The area was a little elevated above the lakeshore, and the lake was visible through the narrow windows on the east side. As we sat, I noticed P becoming very heated. As we gazed at each other in our garb of choice, he simply said, "I'm understanding the wisdom in your choice of clothing." He never did put the suit aside.

Cultural Faux Pas

P and E had a TV and VCR, and we had a large library of tapes, and from time to time, they would ask to borrow a movie. I would make a recommendation, and they would borrow something for the family to enjoy together. I loaned them the *Indiana Jones* trilogy, and a few days later, P returned carrying these movies. He went on and on about the scene in *Temple of Doom* where the meal was served in the palace and exotic dishes were exposed for the guest's enjoyment. As it is in the movie, so it is in Malawi; you do not turn away food that is offered. P described his squeamishness, with great drama, at some of the dishes, and then asked me to consider what it would be like to be invited to a dinner and be served bugs! I laughed and said, "It would be like coming to your house and being served flying ants."

He laughed and replied, "I'd never thought about that." Then he added that great line, "But you've never had them the way my wife prepares them!"

What Falls in the Plate Is Dinner

Yagwa m'bale ndiwo. What falls in the plate is dinner. This brings us to that great missionary prayer: "Lord, I'll eat it if you keep it down." Eating what was set before us was rarely a problem as we were often honored guests. There were, however, those times when either an area or family was particularly poor or the gathering so large we all had to eat from the same bowl. I have to confess, I'm a germophobe. I may be ashamed of it from time to time, but it has served me well, and I was able to stay healthy.

Regardless, there was the time when teaching at the lakeshore had finished in a small village north of Salima, and lunch of small, salted, whole dried fish was served. The smell was pungent to say the least. The shriveled eyes lacked a bit of appeal to my pallet, but I was hungry and a hamburger was nowhere nearby, I'm talking nowhere nearby. So, I ate till I was satisfied and thanked our hosts, who were just happy I did eat.

Then there were the families who would prepare food for the entire community and just invite you. This was especially embarrassing when you know they had spent nearly a month's salary on the meal. We had dear friends do this for us when we had visitors from America. I had told our guests the proper etiquette about refusal to eat. I missed one small detail. When the spread was placed before our guests, the question was asked, "Where's the ketchup?" It may have been harmless or innocent enough, but the bottle of ketchup is another day's wage. It made our host feel they had failed in some way to meet our expectations.

Eat what is set before you without grumbling or complaining.

Who Gives This Woman?

Not long after our arrival in Malawi, we were asked, while relaxing with our employees, which of us owned the children? Who owns the children? I had never thought about it. We said neither Alicia nor I owned our children; we were merely guardians of the children the Lord placed in our care. This was a different concept for those who asked; for you see, depending on the cultural or tribal tradition, you claim either the husband or the family of the wife owns the children. For most of those who lived around us, the wife's family was the owner of the children, which means I would not make decisions for my children. That would be for my wife's oldest brother. Different, huh?

So if a young man came to ask for my daughter's hand, he would not ask me; he would ask my brother-in-law! Then a meeting would be held between representatives of the two families: the family of the young man, and the family of the young woman. The Chichewa word for these family counsellors is very similar to the Chichewa word for "rat." They would agree to the wedding terms and conditions, and perhaps the bride price would be paid to either sell or buy the future children of the couple.

So when I was asked to conduct a wedding at Thonje, the arrangements had been made previously, and P was to officiate, but as per usual, P was away at school. E and the participating families asked me to fill in, which I was only too happy to do. I proceeded in my great nervous tension to get through the ceremony and pronounced them man and wife. All was well but for one small detail. Do you recall in our ceremonies that small part, "Who gives this woman?" Yep, that's the part I forgot, and I was not allowed to forget it either! Yet I still wonder how that question was to be asked. "Have the rats agreed?" is probably how it would have come out.

A Bit of Life in Malawi

What does a missionary do? This is a question we have heard many times. When my parents came for a visit in 1996, my dad summed it up this way: "Now I know what you do! You do exactly what a director of missions does; it just takes you four times longer." In fact, time is consumed with the daily affairs of life that are taken for granted in the United States. For example, while in the States, I have the luxury of paying bills online or perhaps at the checkout of the nearest grocery store, but in Malawi, it is another story. One must visit each utility office to pay the bill from those utilities. Large lines of people form in order to pay their bills. This is just fine for folks who have grown accustomed to negative personal space, but it took some time for me to not feel completely uncomfortable. The bank was my personal favorite. Monday mornings were very busy, especially as businesses wanted to bank what they had brought in over the weekend. I would arrive with others about thirty minutes before the bank opened on Monday morning. When the doors opened, the crowds would rush to the first available teller and keep pressing in until the lobby was shoulder to shoulder, front to back. In these spaces, personal hygiene is noticed.

On one day, I was waiting for my turn at the counter, just like all the other customers, when I heard two ladies behind me talking about the *white man*. "Why does he wait in line?" "Why does he not push up to the front like the other white guys we have known?" "Who is he?" "What is he doing here?" I just listened as the conversation went on. Many in the bank knew me or at least knew that I was attached to the medical clinic, but they said nothing. I decided to join the crowd that said nothing, wanting to hear what may be said.

I finished at the counter and turned to the ladies. I simply greeted them and said, "You never know who can hear you." They were so shocked and became embarrassed. They asked those around them who knew me why they didn't stop them from talking about me if they knew I could understand them. I'll say that was just great fun.

CHAPTER 17

Chiyawo

As A MISSION AGENCY AND as part of a larger global mission outreach effort, we began to reach out to those in our world living in population segments or people groups who did not have an evangelistic outreach or church in their own language. We lived in a Yawo village, but we ministered to the Chewa people of Malawi.

We voluntarily made the decision that we would learn the language of the Yawo people, and when the clinic was officially turned over to the Baptist Convention of Malawi, we would begin our work as church planters among that people group.

When we made that known to many of the Malawians we worked with, the common response we received was, "Why? They deserve to go to hell." Because of the history of the Yawo people partnering with Arab slave traders, the animosity still exists today. The people we had been working with were unwilling to release that history or anger to allow the grace of God to work.

Transition

Regardless of the local attitude, we made the decision to transition into church-planting work, focusing on this vast, unreached Yawo people group among whom we lived. We needed training in the Chiyawo language, and an intense-five week course was set up for mid-August 2001. We were to receive this training at the language institute associated with the University of Zomba in Zomba. We booked a guesthouse run by Catholic sisters in the area. The guesthouse was beautiful, overlooking the rolling hills of the Zomba plateau. Each day we would drive down the mountain for our five hours of language training and then practice. Yet our world was in turmoil.

Each of us who was alive and old enough at the time remembers where we were on September 11, 2001. It was Alicia's birthday, and our fellow missionaries who made their home in Zomba had prepared for the seven of us in the language class and our children to celebrate the evening together. I had left our children in the lodge with their journeyman teacher for the morning as we went to class. After class, I dropped Alicia at our friend's house to prepare for the festivities. I was able to get BBC on the shortwave radio in the car and learned about the attacks on the World Trade Center towers along the way. I collected the children and their teacher, who was on the phone with her mother in Mississippi, getting the horrible updates. When we arrived at the house, I shared the horrible news. At first, Alicia did not believe me. We spent the evening in the lounge at the country club as many from the community filled the room to watch the updates on one of the only televisions in the country.

With growing uncertainty, we were asked to relocate from our isolated location atop the mountain to a more central location where others were already housed. Adjustments had to be made and rooms reassigned, but we moved in with the others in our group late the next evening. During the night, we awoke to a marching army.

We were invaded by a swarm of army ants. They poured down the wall in formation, five across, straight toward Zeb's small bed! We had to evacuate and quickly. These ants leave nothing living and create an odor that fumigates the premises against other insects for months after their visit. As they march, they make an eerie hissing noise, much like a quiet locust. The ants merely added more drama to the events of the week, and it is the one event Zeb remembers from that time.

Short-Lived Expectations

This was all during a relatively short span of time, August 2001 to June 2002. It was a time during which many of our Malawian friends came to us to say, "We heard you were leaving." We had no desire to leave. In fact, we had a pretty clear indication that we would be staying right where we were and begin ministry in a completely new direction. We had finished our short training in Chiyawo. Mrs. Nyika had come to the clinic, and our children were reaching the age where they would be moving on to high school. We had few options with their schooling and the most likely was boarding school at Rift Valley Academy in Kenya. Yet we all began to show signs of something not being right.

We flew to South Africa for some evaluation, and we were called into the educational psychologist's office. We were told our family should find a way to stay together while our children completed their education. Many families do well dealing with children in boarding school and the long periods of separation. I'm not sorry to say our family was not one of these. This started a whirlwind of activity.

Ask and Watch Out

This was a time of uncertainty for our family and ministry. Alicia and I were just talking, and I said, jokingly of course, "Wouldn't it be great if we could get an audible voice from God telling us exactly what to do and where to go?" Well, the roads in Malawi at the time were rough. The drive from our house to our local shopping center in Salima, only twelve miles away, took as long as the drive from Salima to Lilongwe, sixty miles away, due to the very potholed road. After years of driving on roads like this, the radio in our vehicle was coming lose from the antenna, and reception was sketchy at times.

I had just turned off the main road from Salima, headed toward our house on the bumpier sandy access road, when the radio went silent. I was tuned to BBC News at the time. When it came back on, the only word that came through was, "Help," followed again by a break in transmission. When the signal again returned on the next large bump, the radio blasted back to life with only the next few words, "In South Africa," and again deathly silence. No other words came out of the radio that day.

Well, I did ask, didn't I?

Permission Granted

We were visited by member-care folks and encouraged to look for available job openings in the sub-Saharan African region. We made an exploratory trip to South Africa to investigate the area and schooling options. Alicia had made the comment, "Wouldn't it be great if the house was close to the school and the church?" Well, as it turned out, we visited a private Christian school that was exactly the same distance from the house—eight minutes' drive—as the church with the job request. The problem was, if our children were going to enter schooling there, we had to be there no later than June 10. It was mid-May.

We were allowed to transfer to Johannesburg from Malawi for one reason: there was a job there we could fill. The job had been drafted by a local pastor and a fellow colleague. The job was to foster and develop a small group ministry within the life of the church. At least that is how I understood it. The job was rewritten so that we would not be tied to any one church, but I would do church planting and small-group church development throughout all the eastern side of Johannesburg. In consultation with our supervisor at the time, he said we were not bound to this local congregation, but we may want to visit it as the pastor had a hand in writing the request we were filling.

I traveled to the South African embassy in Malawi to submit my application for visa on May 19, with the news from them that the process time would be eight to twelve weeks. So much for the June deadline. Alicia had already begun to pack up the house, but I could not understand why, with no positive word from anyone about the move. I received a call from the South African embassy on May 26 that my application was approved, and we were able to collect our passports at any time. I made the trip that day. What can I say! It was two weeks' notice again! We packed and had to say our last, and less than culturally appropriate, good-byes. We were flying to Johannesburg on the sixth of June. The C. W. McCall song "Convoy" was running through my mind as we made our flight by the light of the moon.

Answered Prayer

Little did we know what kind of spiritual, physical, or emotional shape we would be in when we landed in South Africa, but I began to mourn Malawi. I had gone to Malawi thinking I would serve there until retirement; now that thought was shattered. Though I was drained by Malawi, I did not understand this fact for several months. At the end of that time, a dear friend and elder of the church passed away. I spent the night with my Lord in prayer, and He not only showered me with peace, He brought a healing and vision for new ministry in my life! Before that time, there was so much hurt and bitterness that others could see it in me. After that night, I could not even stir up bitterness or resentment for the pain we experienced there.

I don't know if you have ever experienced walking into a new place and getting the sense of being home. That has happened all along our journey, from Hillside to Mosby and beyond. Well, walking through the doors of Lyndhurst Baptist Church was just like that, I did not need to do any church shopping. Pastor Ian Simms preached a message on that Sunday of our arrival that stirred our hearts and demonstrated his love and commitment to the Word of God. I honestly thought our first Sunday we would see the church vote to oust this pastor for his unashamed stance, but God spared us together for seven very blessed years of life and ministry together in Johannesburg. Pastor Ian has the ability to look deep within you and give you a Word from the Father for just that time. It is an amazing gift he freely shares, and each time he docs it is a great blessing for those who receive it. As a result of his ministry with and to us, we received healing in more ways than one.

I don't know why, but for some reason we all called Ian Simms "Pastor." It just fit, it seemed somehow wrong not to call him Pastor. I cannot explain it, nor do I feel I have to. Ian is Pastor like I, Charles, am Chuck. You know, it just is.

Healing

In January of 2003, I was preparing to eat my cereal and had just pulled the bowl from the cupboard when stroke symptoms hit me. The left side of my body went lame, with no sensation whatsoever. We had guests in the house, and I didn't want my friend to see what was happening to me, so I hobbled back to my bedroom as best I could and from there called for Alicia. When she came into the room, she thought I was playing some kind of game. I must admit that if I were her, I'd think the same thing. My speech was slurred and face droopy. While she was on her way back to the room, the sensation switched sides of my body; it was now the right side that was affected.

Alicia informed our guests she was taking me to the hospital. I was in the bed sleeping when Pastor arrived to see me. He comforted Alicia and told her he would return later. When he returned, I was awake, and instead of asking me how I was, he simply placed his hands on my right knee and prayed. As he did, all the numbness and the buzzing left me. He asked, "How are you feeling?"

I said, "Great! Can I go now?" I did have to wait for the doctor, but the faith of my friend provided healing. I had to stay in hospital for observation and to meet with a neurologist. Glen and Jeri Moore came to stay with us at the hospital while we waited for the doctor to arrive. Glen thought it a good idea to test my cognitive ability by playing a game of Hearts. As we played, a nurse colleague came to keep me company as well. She recognized the doctor when he arrived and told me I should follow him. I caught up with him at the nurses' station and asked if he were looking for Chuck Barrett. He said he was, and I said, "Step into my office," and proceeded into my room. The doctor followed me but went to the other patient in the room with me. I said, "No, doctor, I'm your patient," to which he replied, "No, you're not." After some convincing, he did an examination.

The event set in motion a string of checks and tests: ECG, EKG, MRI, and blood work, all which proved I had both a heart and a brain! I know some of you were wondering … the MRI revealed I had had a previous stroke, which I never noticed. I only discover lost memories when others ask, "Do you remember …?" And I have to say no. Anyway, after all the tests, the doctor's only advice to Alicia was, "If it happens again, just let it pass." Can you imagine?

Through seven years, Ian and I ministered, dreamed, cried, prayed, planned, and ate together. Ian was one of very few national pastors who asked if he could join our evangelistic team as we ministered to a wider area than just his local church setting. He helped us launch efforts to call young people from the United States into service, and he kept us in line when what we were planning would not have been received well in the culture we faced as foreigners. We had a remarkable bond in love and ministry, but nothing on this earth lasts forever.

CHAPTER 18

More People

Al

WE LANDED IN JOHANNESBURG, AND I was clueless—still am most of the time—as to where to start. I was allowed to tag along with a friend who knew the area well and scope out what was happening. He took me way south of Johannesburg to a ministry not tied to any Baptist church, where I met Al and a woman from Brackendowns Baptist Church. It was a few months later that I received a call from this woman for assistance. The ministry was now being directed through Brackendowns Baptist, and she wondered if I would be willing to assist in perhaps expanding the ministry outreach through other church starts. I certainly was!

Over the next six-plus years, Al and I teamed together for encouragement and ministry outreach. You see, the woman from Brackendowns was an early childhood development teacher and trained women in starting and running their own nursery schools (crèche). The schools not only help the children by preparing them for formal education, they help the women by providing a means to support their families. When she would start training, Al and I would follow to check out the spiritual need of the area. Well, okay, Al served as the translator for the both of us. Several Bible studies and outreaches were formed through this effective partnership. Through our time together, I was to learn more of Al's story.

Al was arrested for armed robbery in 1997, and as a result, spent time in prison. He came to faith in Jesus while in prison and was later released on parole. Al's parole officer's life was falling apart, and his wife threw him out of the house. Al lost contact, which was not a good thing for him, but we will get back to that. In the meantime, we had been busy establishing several outreach Bible study groups. One in particular was promising, growing, and needed more full-time assistance. We turned it over to a young man who felt called to ministry, and we were fairly certain he would be faithful. We were greatly disappointed; that promising place just withered as the young man was distracted by other matters of life, and another church group planted a church on the adjoining property. In August of 2007, our friend from Brackendowns called to say she was going to a new, informal settlement area and asked if we would like to join her. We did, and the next week we began teaching in a large, informal area, which seemed to be at the very southwestern edge of this entire region, stretching as far as the eye could see toward the east. It was all close housing and multitudes of people. We met there for about three weeks. When we arrived for the fourth week, the entire place had been bulldozed! I was shocked. Al took it in stride. Al spent the next week searching for the people we had met. In that search, he came across an old friend of his who agreed to let us use his house for a Bible study.

Troubles (Tsietsi)

We started as always with our friend from Brackendowns meeting the women and talking about childcare and education; then we had a group of about twelve stay for Bible study. Each week that number grew to the point that the house could no longer hold us. It was at that point the community leaders came to us and said they were giving us a place, a lot or stand, of our own to build a shack on for meeting. We were grateful. We received the place and began to clean it up. We started to build a shack, and in the midst of that effort, Brackendowns came to dedicate our efforts. So, with three walls up and a tarp for a roof, that morning two were baptized, including Al's sister.

I just have to say, we were in such a hurry to have something up for the dedication that structural stability was not of the greatest importance. The baptistry leaked badly, and I knew it, so I had fifty gallons of water ready to pour in. I thought we were ready, so I instructed those with the water to fill the mud brick baptistry. I don't remember who thought this a good time to say a word, but it was not, and I was losing water! Al's sister nearly missed out. The water never did cover her face. I don't think she was greatly upset.

The next week was Easter, and as I showed up to fetch Al, his sister had told me he had been arrested. *Great. Now what?* were my first thoughts. Shame on me, but I do learn. It seems that after five years of living in the area, the police had finally located this parole violator and were bearing down on him with the full weight of the law. I spent a very lonely, agonizing six months in ministry to *Tsiesti* (problems). I finished the shack, visited Al, and twice a month showed up to court only to have the court file, docket, not show up, and set a date two weeks later. It was a draining time. By the time Al was released, the church had endured the slander of their pastor being a prisoner, but were now rejoicing no wrongdoing was found. The community leader who had provided us the original house for meeting came to Al and me to encourage us to never let anything stand in our way as we ministered in Jesus's name. Al was released in November 2007 and started seminary in January of 2008.

The Easy

Later in 2008, Al approached me to say he wanted to plant another church. I asked if he wasn't busy enough with Tsietsi and seminary, and he assured me that where God leads, He provides. I asked where this place was, and he said he would show me. I brought a couple of guys who were with us, for their semester long missions learning experience, to take a look at this church-planting process. We collected Al and headed to where he believed God was leading him. We saw the place on the highway, but could not get there from where we were. We did manage to find the informal settlement and discovered a large church very close by. I advised Al that it would be wise to see if the large church had any outreach in the area with which we could partner.

We drove into the parking area and started walking toward the church when two men walked out the door. I introduced myself and those with me and asked if they had any outreach into the informal area close by. They looked at each other; one was in a police captain's uniform. They asked for us to reintroduce ourselves. I went through the introductions again, and they looked at each other and at us again. It seems this church had been reaching out into this area for five years and knew it needed to go to the next level, but were stumped at how to take that outreach group to church. They were the elders of this large church and had just left the church after a prayer meeting about this very issue! God is amazing, and His timing is perfect! We spent some time over the next few months getting to know each other, and in December of 2008, I was able to take Al to the informal settlement with a group of volunteers from the States and introduce him as pastor! The members of the community that gathered with us that day began to celebrate what God was doing in their midst! Days like that are rare and thrill the spirit! Al has seen constant struggle with housing and deals with being relocated better than most of us deal with a flat tire. He is and will always be a dear friend and brother.

During our times together, Al and I began outreach works in Polla Park, Thokoza, Tsietsi, Palm Ridge, and there by the highway (I was never there long enough to remember the name). Al even took a volunteer team and me into an all-Zulu area called 'All-Nations' which has been known for its violence. Al knew no fear. Al was and probably still is full of untiring energy for the good news of Jesus Christ. He would often ask me for Bibles during his time in prison. I joked that he was beginning a cell ministry, but he really was making an impact for the Gospel wherever I found him. I'm sure he still is today.

Pastor Ben

I met Pastor Ben through Al. We were scheduled to do some street evangelism and prayer walking through the area I only knew at the time as Thokoza. Al said he knew of a Baptist pastor in the area who would be willing and able to help us with translation and exact locations for the most effective outreach and follow-up. We drove into the area, which was preparing for infrastructure to be installed, and everything looked to be in upheaval. Normally, infrastructure (roads, water supply, sewer, and phone lines) is put in place prior to any houses being started. In the informal settlement areas of South Africa, infrastructure may follow perhaps decades after structures have been in place, and some structures may be built on planned roadways. It was in this mess we stood on a street corner and spoke to all passersby about the good news of Jesus Christ.

It took me time to learn that the area in which Ben lived and ministered was called M'Pumalanga. During Al's imprisonment, Pastor Ben and I began to share more and more time together. We met on Tuesdays for prayer, encouragement, and Bible study, but I was in Tsietsi, just over a mile away, three other days of the week. I grew to know and love Ben's family and the seemingly hundreds of children his wife cared for through their crèche. On one particular Tuesday, as I met with Pastor Ben, he asked when we could go and look for a new place to start a church! As my spirit was throwing a ticker-tape parade, I said, "How about next Tuesday?" It was settled. The next Tuesday arrived, and we loaded into my car and prayed for God's blessing on our efforts. I was hoping it would be close enough that he could do pastoral care through the week, but we drove to the end of the road, six miles south to Thula Sizwe. The meaning of *Thula Sizwe* can be twofold. One interpretation is "hush, be still," with the understanding that you are about to receive instruction. The second meaning is simply, "hush; stop your crying." Thula Sizwe is just a small smattering of houses and shacks that has been in place for fifty years to service the nearby farm. We know because we asked residents who had lived there that long. The one change over that time is the water tank that was erected in the center of the houses, which is filled weekly by the local counsel.

As you arrive in a new place, you must first seek approval from the community leader to be there; it is true all over sub-Saharan Africa. So the plan was to look for that person first. We pulled up close to the water tank and opened our car doors to exit the vehicle. Pastor Ben was immediately face-to-face with a young man, who simply stated, "I need Jesus." Experience has taught both of us to be very wary in new environments. He had a chat with the young man, who made a profession of faith in Jesus Christ as his Lord, and Ben sent him to me for discipleship material, which I normally carried.

As soon as the young man was with me, Pastor Ben was confronted by a young woman, who made the statement, "I need what he asked for too." We had still not yet received permission for our presence. After I had finished with the young man, who spoke excellent English, I went exploring a bit until Ben motioned to say, "Come assist the young lady with material as well." In my exploration, I found I could not communicate with any of the older people in the area. I discovered an elderly woman who had not the strength so sit, talk, or feed herself. As I watched, there seemed to be some sort of line forming of people waiting to speak with Ben. About fifth in the line was another woman of middle age, and she approached him to say, "If you need a place to hold Bible study, you can use my house." We never did get permission to be there, but over the next several months, we held Bible study at that large blue shack next to the water tank.

As a side story, the lady who was so sickly was prayed for weekly. She began to recover to the point of sitting up, feeding herself, and talking. I discovered she was either 106 or 99 years of age. She was being looked after by a daughter and daughter-in-law from Lesotho. I was finally alone with her for just a moment where we could discuss her faith and her certainty of where she would spend eternity. She assured me of her salvation through Christ and told me she was ready to go; that I could please stop praying for her healing, but that I would make her a good son-in-law. We shared a good laugh that Tuesday. She passed away the same week, two days later. It was at her funeral we discovered another couple interested in starting a church in the area. They were an older couple, but Thula Sizwe was the woman's childhood home, and now she and her husband were back to establish a church.

Pastor Ben and I offered our assistance if needed but gave them our blessing as we could see they wanted to be faithful to the Word of God, and we were not in competition. Sometimes it takes years to find anyone faithful enough to take up the work of the Lord that has started in an area. We realized what a blessing this couple was, and those who were being faithful in our times together were growing to the point that they could be a church together and continue to grow.

The next week, Ben asked where we were going next. Not having a clue myself, I trusted his knowledge of the area. I did request it be closer this time to allow for better pastoral care for when a car is not available. It was not closer. Each week we passed by Thula Sizwe on the road to Somalia, some fifteen miles away. Funny thing this, from Ben's home, we could see Zonke Sizwe, or "all the nations," and travel to Somalia in a matter of minutes. Anyway, Somalia is simply an informal settlement: no toilets, no electricity or water to the houses, just outside water spigots every one hundred yards or so. If you ever travel in South Africa from Johannesburg to Durban by car, Somalia is just off the left side of the road. It's the last cluster of shacks as you pass over the Vosluroos exit. We met in the big dark blue shack.

On one of our first visits to Somalia, a man several houses down called out, "Hello, Pastor!" I knew Ben was well-known and respected in the area, but I was still surprised. As we were meeting, the man arrived for Bible study sporting the jacket of a nearby hotel where we often held mission meetings. I asked him about it, and he said, "Yes, I work there. I remember you prayed for me the last time you were there." We had indeed, and I was reminded of my place—that there is no place for an ambassador of the King to hide, no place where inappropriate is acceptable.

Prayer-Walking

Thokoza was the major area of my focus while in South Africa. It is large and crowded spreading 25 miles to the east and I learned Thokoza was just the name for one bit of the western section. One of the first lessons I learned, thanks to the help of Pastor Guy De Swart and a volunteer team headed by Michael Richards from Chattanooga, Tennessee, was that of prayer-walking. First, it is necessary to know you are in battle when entering an area to establish a church. If you don't think it's real, try it. We spent the first day or two watching doors and curtains close before we ever approached a house. And then, though folks knew we were there, they would not answer.

After these first two days, we were discouraged and wondered what was happening. We parted company for the night, and we each lifted the matter in prayer. The next morning, the answer came to me: we needed to spend time in the area just praying. I thought, *No one is going to be interested in just praying. We want to see people come to faith, and that involves speaking to people.* Nevertheless, I was convinced in my spirit this was of the Lord. But how to share the news with the others?

As I arrived at the guesthouse where the team was staying, I stepped out of the car for a morning chat, when their team leader came to me and said, "We believe we just need to pray today, and I had to get it out before you shared your plans with us." Wow! That was easy. They shared that as a team, they were each led to the same conclusion: that we were to spend the day walking around the area and praying for the community. Cool; now to inform Pastor Guy.

You can guess, as we arrived and met Guy, the first thing out of his mouth was, "Folks, I believe we need to spend the day in prayer around the community." When the Spirit is clear ...

We prayed, and after only one day of prayer-walking and praying God's power and peace over the area, folks were coming out of their houses to meet us and ask why we were there. This is the same area where just weeks before, Guy and I were on a visit and felt at the same moment a sense of discomfort and an urgent need to leave the area; a police helicopter had begun to hover over us and stayed with us until we left.

As the team prayed through the area, we found four young men playing a game of cards in their drive, and we each felt a particularly dark spirit as we passed. Throughout the week, we prayed, and specifically on the corner by that house. On our last day in the area, the men were again out in their drive, preparing goat heads for supper. In order to allow them to hear the message, I took over some of the preparation work, which took them by surprise. They were more than happy to sit and listen to the team's testimonies. By the time we were leaving, the heads were finished and they had heard the good news of Jesus! This church was well looked-after by Boksburg Baptist Church. As I was leaving South Africa in 2009, I went to visit the church and their pastor in their new steel-framed building.

Release!

Prayer-walking was from then on the first priority in our new outreach center strategy. While on such a prayer-walk in Pastor Ben's area, we came to a shipping container where children were playing outside. A door and window had been cut out to make it a usable shack. We introduced ourselves and presented the Gospel to the owner, who quickly asked if we would share this message with the one who looked after the children. I don't know if you have ever been in a shipping container, but there is not a lot of space. In this room—eight feet wide, eight feet tall, and twenty feet long—there was modest seating and four of us with these two ladies. The children's caretaker came and sat on the arm of the chair as we talked. We introduced ourselves, and she immediately piped in, "You don't need to share anything with me. I belong to the Sangoma (the traditional healer)."

I asked if I could ask her some questions because I was curious how that all worked. She agreed to answer my questions, and I began, "So, if you do something wrong and want to make it right, what do you do?"

"Oh," she said, "that's easy. I go to the Sangoma, and he tells me to bring him two chickens."

"And then?" I asked.

"Well, and then he takes the chickens out back and cuts their throats," she replied.

"And then?"

"And the blood covers my sin." (Her words exactly; no translation needed.)

"What if I could tell you about a blood that would cover all your sins once and for all?"

"Oh, I'd like that!"

I have told you the size of this shipping container. It became smaller when she heard the good news of God's love and forgiveness available through Jesus's blood. When she received His forgiveness and made Him her Lord, she was rejoicing so greatly. She was free from the power of sin!

There were many who came to faith: some dramatic and some not so much. But I never encountered anything like this before or since.

CHAPTER 19
Carjacking(s)

One

I DO HAVE TO SHARE some stories of the not-so-nice variety. We lived in a nice house in Jo'burg, located near the area where two major thoroughfares come together. It was also close to Alexandra, a particularly populated area of town known for some violence. We drove a type of vehicle that was susceptible to carjackings, but it was the perfect family car. As Alicia was pulling out of the drive one morning, going to assist Zeb's class as they went on an outing, two men, at least one with a gun, ran up to her and demanded the car. She wisely stepped away, and they took the vehicle. One of our neighbors was on her balcony—we lived next to a set of three-story apartments—and saw the whole encounter. What we did not know was that she was a counsellor for one of the local police departments. As the carjacking was taking place, she was on her cell phone making the call to the police and asked for the helicopter to assist in recovering our vehicle. She described our vehicle, the men, and the direction they left in as the events unfolded.

Alicia was left standing in our drive with no way back into the house, as they had taken her keys and she had locked the security gate on her way out. We lived in a bird cage in a fortress. With nowhere else to go, she ran to our friends, a husband and wife team who ran a hairdressing salon on the corner. The husband headed to our house, forty yards away, jumped the fence, and began to bang on the door with his fist. I was in the back of the house taking a shower. When he found me, he yelled through the closed window that Alicia had been carjacked. She was all right and at their shop, but shaken a bit. I think it may have worried him when I decided to finish my shower before joining them in their worry. God is and was in control.

Friends arrived moments before the police and assisted me in accompanying them to find the vehicle. I think we still hold some kind of record: vehicle stolen and recovered in less than twenty-five minutes. I was able to talk to the helicopter pilot who found the vehicle driving through Alexandra. He loves his job and said it is so great to find a vehicle, hover over it, and watch the thieves scatter. All this because one neighbor cared. How much pain and suffering can we help our neighbors avoid if we care?

Ian Simms was at our house in short order and asked if this would be an event that would scare us enough to send us home or off the mission field or out of South Africa. He spent some time with us in pastoral care, and we assured him of God's call on our lives and our comfort in the fact that He had orchestrated our transition to South Africa. Zeb remembers the event as "those men stole my lunch, and my friends shared their lunches with me."

Two

Alicia had taken Barnabas and Sarah to their ACT testing and was dropping Sarah at a friend's house to spend the night. It was a gated community, so we felt fairly confident Sarah was going to be fine. The gates were raised at the entrance of the community, and Alicia went through. She noticed she was being followed, so she continued to drive around the area before pulling into the drive at the house. The car that had been following, no longer in sight, suddenly appeared around the corner and parked behind Alicia. It was enough of a lag time that Sarah was retrieving her things from the back of the car and was frozen there as the drama unfolded. One of the men quickly notice Barnabas and hit him with a cupped hand over the right ear, causing pain and disorientation. The car was surrendered with Sarah's overnight luggage and both Barnabas's and Sarah's passports, which they needed for the ACT, as well as Alicia's handbag.

This was a traumatizing time for our two children. We were able to retrieve the car from the police impound in Soweto. The car had basically been stripped, and there was no way of telling when and where the damage was done. Again Ian was at the house shortly afterward with the same questions: would this be the event that took us from the mission field?

Three

Only four months later, I wanted to visit some couples from the church, but I was not sure which couple to visit first, thinking I could make both visits in one evening. As I needed to make a short stop at the church first, I could make the decision later. At the church, one of our youth asked if I would not mind giving him a lift home. That made the decision of which couple to visit first easy, as one couple lived across the street. It was still not too late; the sun was shining and a large group was playing soccer close to where I had parked. Though I set no time limit, it was dark by the time I went to the car. I had to clear three security doors before leaving the complex of the first visit. As I approached the car, I released the door locks, which prompted two men standing at the next set of apartments to run at me, one wielding a gun.

I really tried the back-away strategy that seemed to work so well for Alicia, but the man with the gun was insistent. So much was going through my mind: *Is this gun real? Is it the only one? Is it loaded?* At some point, I remember surrendering, and the realization struck me that though I was taken by surprise by these men, God was not at all surprised. I prayed in that moment, "Okay, Lord. You know what is going on. I trust you." With that, I simply followed every other instruction given. I was told to get into the back seat and lace my fingers around the headrest of the front seat. I was told not to look up or look at them.

The man giving the instruction was extremely nervous and he used excessive amounts of profanity. Perhaps the gun was not real. I told him he didn't need to curse at me; he had me and the vehicle. To this, the driver said, "You need to calm down."

The fellow with the gun then jabbed it farther into my side and repeated the phrase, "See there, you need to calm down."

This evoked laughter from me; sorry, that was funny. He asked why I was laughing. I told him, "I think he's talking to you." He assured me it was not a good idea to laugh at him. I didn't again.

My thoughts were still racing, and still do as I write. It is nearly unheard of to be hijacked and live. I recalled all my most recent conversations with Alicia, each of my children, and friends, in the event of my demise, all was good. I would leave no one with anger and perhaps little unresolved. I was told they knew where I lived, and if I tried anything, they would kill my family. Their ignorance of their espoused knowledge was clear as they were driving me closer to my house and not away from it, hoping to get me confused as to my location.

When they gave me an opportunity to exit the vehicle, I didn't give them a second chance. I ran just far enough to hear them speeding away. I was left only a mile from the house, but they had relieved me of my cell phone, wallet, wedding ring, keys, and the prized pen Dad had made for me from my grandfather's barn wood. It was dark, and two men walked in my direction. I asked if either had a cell phone I could use to call the police, that my car had been hijacked. They jokingly said, "It looked as if it was driven like it had been stolen," to which we all laughed. As we met in the middle of the road, a cell phone was handed to me with the local police station on the other end of the line! I relayed my story and was assured that an officer was on the way. By the time the call was over, we had walked to a main road and I had run my rescuer out of prepaid time on his cell phone.

The street was well traveled and close to home, I told my two companions I may as well walk home; the police surely would not find me where I was. We had another good laugh, and I turned to go. I had no more than stepped off the curb when a police vehicle rolled around the corner and the officer on the passenger side stepped out, drew his pistol, and ordered us all to halt. We looked at each other in amazement. I guess he had never seen two black guys in the willing company of a white guy before. We assured him I had just been hijacked and the two men now in my company were helping me. The policeman quickly changed his stance and offered his assistance.

They loaded me into the front of the vehicle, which was a squeeze, and began to radio in that they had a Mr. Barrett they were taking to the local police station for a report. Not five seconds later came the report that was made as a result of my hijacking: "Be on the lookout for …" The officer again picked up his radio and began to explain they had Mr. Barrett and were transporting him to the local police station. It was at this point the dispatcher lost all sense of protocol. "What did you say?" was the question that came back. The officer explained again, and the dispatcher simply said, "Okay."

I arrived at the Bramley Police Station perhaps twenty or thirty minutes after I disappeared from my friend's sight. I do have to say, it was fairly traumatic for the wife of the couple I was visiting as she watched all the events of the carjacking taking place, for which I am sorry. In the meantime, Ian Simms had called Alicia and asked if he could pay a visit to our house. The call for prayer had gone out, and Ian wanted to be with Alicia and not have her receive word through the phone.

I reached the police station and was asked to sit in the main area to wait. The vehicle that had brought me was from my local area, but I was hijacked in another precinct, and that is where the report needed to be filed. I sat until someone wondered why a lone man was sitting in the lobby. I was asked if I needed help. It was then they discovered I was the man they were all busy looking for.

I was taken back into another room with a large window that faced the parking lot to give my statement. I asked if I could call my wife before I spoke to them. Ian and Alicia had just said, "Amen," when the phone rang. I was in the process of making my statement when I noticed the officer's face grow with concern. Some of our youth received the call, and having no fear, had left their house to rescue me. It was this group of young men that now appeared in the parking lot of the police station, and the eldest was quickly making his way to my aid. I only noticed them when the officer's concern grew to an alarming point and I had to turn to see. The officer asked if I knew this man as I stood to hug S'fiso. I assured him I did; he was my nephew. In South Africa, I was known as Uncle Chuck, so I asked S'fiso who I was in front of the officer. S'fiso responded with, "Uncle Chuck."

So I looked at the officer and said, pointing to myself, "Uncle Chuck." Then pointing to S'fiso, I said, "Nephew." The officer was not so amused.

After this incident, I needed counseling as I had felt those were to be my last hours on the earth. Ian provided that counseling and asked if this would be the event that sent us home. I assured him it would not.

CHAPTER 20

Australia

OUR PASTOR ANNOUNCED HE WAS being pursued by a church in Australia and our time together was coming to an end. He had preached a series of sermons some time earlier on sifting, and we as a church experienced that sifting as our church administrator left to care for her father and our youth pastor left to advance his education and pursue missions; he is now pastor. We, as a church, had been prepared for spiritually going after God in times of change and even adversity, but Ian was a friend too; those are few and far between, and we had enjoyed ministry together. As Pastor was leaving, he was preparing me to receive the lion's share of a ministerial load. The church was looking to me for pastoral guidance and asked if I would chair the call committee as we looked for a new pastor. Pastor left in February of 2009, but not before he made a brief statement about sensing our time of ministry together was not finished. I was leaving for a year in America in June, and the church wanted God's man in place before I left. I love my job. After what seemed like a long search, a man recently returned from Italy as a missionary— who had grown up in the church and whose mother was part of the congregation—accepted the call. He was voted in as pastor on our last Sunday in Johannesburg. Whew!

As we were leaving Johannesburg in 2009, there was so much on our minds. Our church family—especially the leadership folks—and I use *family* for we were and are that close—came to us and expressed their thanks for the years of service in the life of the church. But they felt the Lord leading us on, and our time together was finished. We did not quite know what to think. Strange, that. Pastors Ben and Al both expressed the same sentiment. The pastors in the churches in the southeastern part of Johannesburg, around Thokoza, caught a vision for the work of church planting throughout the Thokoza area and were glad to share that with their churches as a vital part of mission outreach. The small groups Alicia and I were leading had been being led by individuals who knew their time to step up into leadership had come. All this to say that everything we were involved in had been received by others, making our exit seem complete and leaving us wondering where we would go when we returned to Johannesburg.

We had previously planned to be the missionaries-in-residence at Oklahoma Baptist University, and we were excited about the opportunity. (I would encourage any colleague to take advantage of such an opportunity.) We were hoping to be with our college-age children as they adjusted to life in the United States and give insight to the college students who may be pursuing missions upon graduation. It was toward the end of 2009 when we heard through the grapevine that the mission was selling the house in which we had lived for the past seven years. That was not a problem; it just reinforced a change in ministerial direction. In the mix of things, we heard our outreach efforts would take on new focus upon our return. It was not good or bad, just different. I cannot point to one event or a single thing that confirmed in our hearts that we would not return to ministry in South Africa; it was just a combination of many small things that made that point clear. It was perhaps first clear to those with whom we ministered.

In the personal confusion of the time, knowing we would leave children behind as we returned to the field, I sent out a total of four resumes to some area churches looking for a pastor. We were not cashing in our missions calling; we just wanted to know the will of

God. We shared all that was happening with those close to us in Shawnee and asked if they would pray with us.

During this time, we found a church looking for a pastor in a town exactly forty-two miles from each parent—God's provision. I mean, what could be more perfect than something exactly equidistant to both parents. We decided to travel to the city and do some scouting (snooping) around. We looked on the internet for houses located in the city and found the perfect house. Let me spell this out: *the perfect house*! This house had a two-car garage, with room on the ground floor for a granny flat so Alicia's mom could live with us or at least stay in comfort without having stairs to navigate. This house had four bedrooms and three bathrooms, an in-ground swimming pool, and a hot tub. It had a privacy fence around the pool as well as a large garden all around. In the back, the house bordered a drop-off along the rail line, so no one was ever going to build behind the house. At the end of the street, which was half a block down, was a large state fish hatchery! It was the perfect house in the perfect place. But wait! There is more! In that economy, this house, with all its amenities, was listed at ninety-four thousand dollars! God's call, yes? Of the resumes we sent out, we heard back from only one. That's right, that exact church, said no. What was God up to?

One whole week passed by, and we were open to hear God's voice that the church had changed its mind and was asking us to come preach in view of a call. I even called Dad to tell him I had sent out my resume to stay closer. Dad cut right to the chase; he has that way and that freedom. "You need to find where God is leading and follow," he said. "You and I both know you will not be fulfilled being a pastor here."

Then, after that week, we received a call from Ian Simms. "Would we consider a move to Australia?" Wow! We never had Australia in mind.

With all the changes in South Africa and our wondering what was next, this call from Australia had not been in our wildest dreams.

When we were first married, we had romantic thoughts of living in Australia, but our efforts of finding employment there turned to up empty. So we knew that if these new doors were to open, it would be of the Lord. The IMB had at one time a comity agreement with the Baptist Union of Australia. These simply say this will be where you work, and we will leave it to you. Thus we knew there were few in Australia who entered with the IMB. We were frank with Ian that it would be a waste of his time and energy to pursue a request that we transition to Australia, but he was adamant. We would need approval from the IMB and Baptist Union of Churches in Western Australia, the mother church where Ian was pastor, and the church re-plant along with approval from the state of Western Australian. They would all have to be in agreement regarding the job and my capacity to fill it. Along with these hurdles were those within the IMB regarding the transfer of personnel from one field of service to another. So many roadblocks could be thrown up by any of these groups at any time, it was just not worth the headache.

Ian initiated the process as he had done in South Africa. Our initial feedback was positive from all who received word about the possibility. All throughout the process, we were affirmed by family, friends, colleagues, and those involved. The Baptist Union of Churches of Western Australia even agreed to sponsor our visa! Amazingly, in the process of things, we received a five-year visa! You may wonder why this is so amazing. The religious worker's visa is a two-year visa. God is so amazing, and we are so blessed.

We had the privilege of seeing amazing things happen. We needed a police clearance letter from South Africa. It is common to be in the country to make such a request, and we needed this document as a requirement for the Australian visa process purposes. I found a South African consulate website, followed the instructions listed, and sent the needed paperwork to, of course, Glen Moore, who submitted the request with no problems. Not a minor thing.

We submitted our paperwork and heard nothing in the time frame that was set forth by the Australian embassy. Alicia called simply to enquire. The woman on the other end of the line said how glad she was that we called, as she had been trying to reach us and did not have our correct address. We were then informed we also required an FBI clearance letter. This, we were told, would take some eight to twelve weeks. The folks in Perth, Australia were waiting, just as we were. The clearance came early!

We submitted the FBI clearance to Australian authorities, and within days, our approval for the religious worker's visa came through. We were quick to contact the travel folks for the IMB. We were planning to fly out after the first of the year so that our older children would be back in school and we could leave them settled rather than leaving them while they were still on mid-year break. Because we had to travel to Johannesburg to pack our furnishings for transport to Australia, our flights were scheduled to maximize time and minimize cost. Also, as I did not want to travel to Australia by myself, and Alicia and Zeb didn't want to reach Australia without me, we were willing to pay the difference in prices to travel to Johannesburg and then Perth together. Those arrangements were being made for mid-January 2011 when we received a call. We could save enough money on tickets that we would pay no difference, but there was a catch. You, got it, two weeks' notice!

As I prepared to leave two of my three children in the States to return to the mission field, my heart was torn as my father-in-law's must have been.

And the stories continue …

Printed in the United States
By Bookmasters